FINDING MARTIANS
IN THE DARK

FINDING MARTIANS IN THE DARK

Everything I Needed to Know About Teaching Took Me Only 30 Years to Learn

DAN M. BIEBEL

Healthy Life Press
Roseland, Florida

FINDING MARTIANS IN THE DARK

Copyright © 2010, 2013 by Dan M. Biebel, and
Healthy Life Press, 2603 Drake Drive, Orlando, FL 32810
www.healthylifepress.com

Cover design by Judy Johnson

Printed in the United States of America

Library of Congress Cataloging-in-Publication Data

Biebel, Dan
  Finding Martians in the Dark: Everything I Needed to Know About Teaching Took Me Only 30 Years to Learn

ISBN 978-1-9392-6716-0

1. Teaching; 2. Teacher Education

Published by Healthy Life Press. Most Healthy Life Press resources are available worldwide through bookstores and online outlets, depending on their format. This book also exists in a downloadable and printable PDF from www.healthylifepress.com. Multiple copy discounts may be arranged by contacting the publisher at the address above, or by e-mailing: info@healthylifepress.com. Copying or distributing printed or eBook formatted books or portions thereof is a violation of international copyright law, and strictly forbidden.

Names of characters mentioned in the stories that follow have been changed to protect the privacy and reputation of people who have been associated with the author in his lifelong search for "Martians" hiding in hedges just about everywhere he has lived.

DEDICATION

I dedicate this book to all teachers everywhere
who somehow find the time to analyze and
question why they do what they do,
and how they do it,
invoking a sense of humor in the process,
with the goal of making things
better for kids.

ACKNOWLEDGEMENTS

Thanks be to Maryke Nel for encouraging me to continue writing when I was beginning this work in the early 1990s and to my brother Dave Biebel for encouraging, and helping me finish it, in 2010.

A deep appreciation is sent out to all of my present and former administrators and colleagues who gave me the space I needed to develop as a teacher, and especially those who were willing to "chew the fat" for hours about the world of education, leading to most of the thoughts in this book.

In particular, I have to thank colleagues and friends: Rick Newton, Wayne Roadifer, John Tinnin, Chuck Wells, Mila Stender, Rick Scherry, David Harris, Art Orr, Jeff Poulsen, Jack Steinhorst, and my wife, Cheri, for their insights, wisdom, and sense of humor, which helped inspire me in this project. You are all good role models for me and you have contributed to and blessed my life and the lives of your students more than you will ever know.

A special place in my heart has always been occupied by my heroes who have had a lasting, positive influence on me, particularly Coach John Barth, Marion Graham, and my Dad, more because of what they did and who they are than by what they said.

P.S. Thanks to all my awesome students who made me look good.

INTRODUCTION

In the early 1990s, I was filling my coffee cup in the teachers' lounge prior to the start of school one fall day when my principal asked me if I was interested in "taking on" a student teacher for the next semester.

"Sure, why not?" I said. "Sounds like fun." As I looked at the fresh coffee stain on my shirt, I thought maybe the first important lesson should be in the appropriate technique of handling coffee cups, especially the avoidance of stains on clothing, lesson plans, student papers, and gradebooks, all of which I need to practice myself.

For the next few weeks it occurred to me that the best thing for the upstart, talented, creative, energetic youngster (and the two that followed soon after) might be if I disappeared as much as possible so they didn't pick up any of my other bad habits. Having wrestled with this temptation and lost, I spent three semesters as a student-teacher "supervising teacher," which was very rewarding.

As these student teachers took on more responsibilities, I was beginning to wonder about what it was that I should be passing on to them. I wondered if there was any "teacher stuff" that I could share that could keep them from having to learn the "hard way." Also, at the same time, I was picking up on some of their less "old school" ways of thinking. All of this set me on a journey of introspection that still hasn't ended.

While they were fully in control of my classes, I began to vent these thoughts on paper, trying to organize and connect them with some of my life's experiences as a way of making sense of it all. I was trying to connect what I was doing, and not doing, with who I am as a person, trying to be careful not to take myself too seriously.

Although the book is not in exact chronological sequence, the stories from my childhood derive from my upbringing in Windsor, Vermont, where I graduated from high school in 1970. Most of the other stories come from experiences that occurred while teaching and coaching at rural schools in north central Wyoming from 1977 to 2003.

Nineteen years later, after a long break in the middle, a journey if you will, I went through another time of similar need, a time to express thoughts that reflect on the journey of a teaching career as it nears the end. This time, from 2003 to the present, while teaching in south Florida, is when the final chapters were written.

As I reflect on the work to follow, I see the story of a teacher who ran the race, a marathon, with times of exhilaration, frustration, joy, fear, anger, contentment, satisfaction, confusion, love, and a sincere desire to make a difference in the world.

It's complicated, this teacher thing.

This book is intended to expose all of these emotions, mix them with humor, and hopefully give readers something to ponder as they pass along a similar path.

–Dan M. Biebel
February 2010

CONTENTS

1

Beginnings

It happened one bright spring day in the middle of May. I was sitting in Freshman English class during sixth period, counting the length of time I could hold my breath, and challenging my nearby neighbors to beat my time. This technique was part of my repertoire of techniques for making it through lengthy church services as well. Here at school, in this particular class, most of us were good students, but what we really wanted was the time to be passing faster so we could get outside to play baseball, which was our rite of spring. All the boys in this Vermont town loved baseball, especially on a glorious day like this one. Little did I know that the course of my life would be determined in the next couple of minutes.

Up front, Mrs. Grantham was expounding on the virtues of English grammar, particularly the value of knowing the difference between an adjective and an adverb. "Okay, class," she said, "remember, an adverb modifies a verb, and an adjective modifies a noun."

Ho-hum, I thought, *like the solid brown bat hit the solid white ball solidly.* I figured I knew enough about this adverb/adjective thing already, and was starting on another one of those out-of-the-body experiences (which would hopefully take me across the bridge over Mill Brook to MacLeay Field, where we played ball).

These out-of-the-body experiences had occurred a lot lately, and this time I found myself floating up to the ceiling, where I could see the whole class below me. There was a person that looked just like me, although I hadn't noticed him before, beginning to snore loudly enough to make the students around him giggle. Mrs. Grantham, who never put up with snoring above 60 decibels, starting moving in the direction of the culprit. I chuckled to myself, since I knew what was about to happen. I had been the brunt of more than one of her tirades before, and knew what this poor fellow had gotten himself into. It would have been a really good show, except that Frank Shelton, who normally sat behind me, kicked the poor guy in the derriere just before she got there.

I'm not sure what happened after that because I was unceremoniously sucked back into my body without warning. As I looked up, there was Mrs. Grantham standing over me, and I knew I had something to worry about. I looked behind me. Frank Shelton had a big smirk on his face. I wondered how he got there so fast and was about to ask him, but, by the look on Mrs. Grantham's face, I thought maybe it could wait 'til the bell rang.

Mrs. Grantham, or "Storm Force Grantham," as she was affectionately called by those of us who knew her at the deeper level, was just about to unleash the full force of her wrath on me, when there was a knock on the door and the principal's secretary, Mrs. Reinhardt, opened it. "Mrs. Grantham, you're wanted in the office," she said.

I looked heavenward, now knowing for sure that there was a God. (and promising to stop the breath-holding in church). Mrs. Grantham looked around to see who she was going to leave in charge. With only the slyest look on her face she said, "Okay, Biebel, you're in charge here. And since you obviously know about adjectives and adverbs, get up front and see what you can do about helping some of your classmates who don't."

And then she hustled out the door. I distinctly remember hearing a sinister cackling laughter after the door shut, similar to the witch in the *Wizard of Oz*.

I knew I had looked heavenward a little too soon. Sometimes I think God has a wry sense of humor--well, at least as it applies to me. I slowly made my way to the front of the classroom. I was a little scared, and all my friends didn't look nearly as friendly as they should have. I wasn't quite sure what to say, so I just started, hoping that it would be like running downhill or jump-starting a motorcycle.

"Okay," I said, "who's having trouble with adjectives and adverbs?" Again I looked heavenward, hoping for better results this time. *Please let no one answer*, I prayed silently. No one did.

Then I took the workbook out and started going over the assignment, which consisted of identifying underlined words in sentences as being either adverbs or adjectives. "Let's see how the assignment went for everyone," I said. "Okay, Frank," (I picked out Frank because I knew he would know the right answer, an important technique that I have kept in my teaching skill set since.) What did you get for the first sentence?" So I went on around the class, picking out the bright kids so I wouldn't have to answer anything too tough, until I got to Susan.

"Okay, Susan, what did you get for number thirteen?" I asked.

"I didn't get it," she whispered. "Fact is, I haven't gotten one of these questions right, and I can't figure it out."

I should have seen the warning signs. She was fidgeting all over her chair and nervously playing with her pencil. She looked like she might cry at any second. It was too late to offer her a bathroom pass so she could hide out down there until the bell rang. I felt sorry for her.

Oh boy, I thought to myself, *now I've done it.*

The boys would never let me forget this one once we got out on the field. I could hear 'em already, "Hey, Bieb, nice teaching. Maybe you need to learn how to sleep with your eyes open next time!" There would be no letup. I looked at the clock, thinking someone must have forgotten to ring the bell, but there were ten minutes left.

"Okay, Susan," I heard myself saying with feigned (and also unbelievable) confidence, "you can handle this. Let's read the sentence." I read the sentence to her. "The large brown bear was angrily approaching the hunter." *Reminds me of a certain teacher who had just approached my desk in like manner*, I thought. In the workbook, both "large" and "angrily" were underlined.

"Okay, which one of those two words modifies the noun, bear?" I asked. She looked at me. I could see that she was home, but the lights weren't on. She didn't have it.

"Try it this way," I begged. "Which of the two underlined words describes the bear, and which one describes how he approaches?"

Suddenly, it was if New England Power and Light had turned on full power all at once and flooded her mind. "Oh," she exclaimed, "I get it! Can I try the next one?" Susan tried the next one and the next, proving that she did, indeed, have it.

I was amazed for two reasons: First, that she had emerged from the dark after one simple question; Second, because I felt so good about having been part of it.

I felt like I had just been up to bat in the last inning of a baseball game with the bases loaded, two outs, and our team behind by three runs, and had come through with a grand slam. I was nervous, for some reason, and excited, and proud, all at the same time.

Mrs. Grantham returned to the room shortly thereafter, and I returned to my seat, this time very much awake. "I guess you learned what it was like to be a teacher and how to stay awake, didn't you?" she queried with that same sly look on her face.

"Yes, ma'am," I said. I was feeling really good. I knew then that I would never forget the look in Susan's eyes when the lights came on, and I'd never forget the satisfaction I had felt, knowing that I had flipped the switch.

More than forty years have passed since that day in Freshman English. I have wondered many times if my life would have been different had I not fallen asleep in class that particular day. I'm glad it happened, for I learned that day that I was destined to be a teacher. I knew what my niche was going to be.

I worry about some of my friends who never did seem to find out what they should become. I wonder how many "born" teachers never discovered that they had the gift. Maybe more young students need to fall asleep in class so they can learn what I did that day.

I also have wondered at times how many people knew they had

the gift and didn't use it, for whatever reasons. I feel sorry for them. They've missed out on a wonderful experience, one that is replete with completeness and the knowledge that they are doing something with lasting significance, leaving a piece of themselves in the lives of everyone who passes through their classroom.

I don't teach so much because I want to. It really is more than that. *I teach because I have to.* I still feel the same satisfaction today that I felt on that spring day in 1967, and I know that happiness ties in with the gift and the proper use of it.

Being a teacher is one of the highest of callings. Everyone should feel that way about their career; otherwise, it's just a job.

If I had to do it over again, I'd do it over again.

· · · · · · · · · 2 · · · · · · · ·

The Natural

It was the first day of track practice on a beautiful warm, sunny day in March. Being not only the coach but a track buff of the first order as well, I was expecting the entire student body to join the team and was trying to figure out how to convince the athletic director to buy more uniforms and schedule more track meets. After everyone had congregated, I realized that I may have exaggerated in my prediction a bit. We had what amounted to an enviable student-teacher ratio in any classroom--eight kids had signed up for track.

I was devastated at first, but I knew that some of the athletes had ability because I had seen them play basketball, so we started practice. We jogged and stretched and did "buildup sprints." Then we discussed matching events with various kids' talents, trying to avoid uncomfortable situations where a sundial might be needed to time one of them in an event that would maybe embarrass them. So, the plan was to see who could jump and sprint and then try and develop the others into weight people and distance runners. I sent them all down to the long jump pit, the high jump, and the pole vault pit. I supervised the pole vault, because if anyone tried to kill themselves I would be negligent not to be there and watch it happen.

As practice progressed, one of the kids approached me and yelled, "Hey, Coach! Jeff just long-jumped 19 feet." Jeff was a freshman, so I thought I'd better make sure they were measuring with the right side of the measuring tape. I hurried over to the long jump pit, which amounted to a long dirt path leading to a hole in the ground filled with sand. Jeff was preparing to jump again, and I watched him at the end of the runway. He was in a half crouch, one leg in front of the other, kind of coiled up like a rattlesnake about to strike. When he was sure I was watching, he sprinted down the runway, hit the takeoff board perfectly, leaped high in the air, sailed out and landed, textbook style, in the pit about 19 feet from the board.

Now 19 feet is not a "Carl Lewis" type jump, mind you, but if you're a high school track coach in a very small high school, you can get excited about a freshman prospect like that. Like a jeweler who had just come upon an unpolished gem, wanting to hone it down and get every last ounce of beauty out of it, I studied the long jump. I learned everything I could about it: approach run, takeoff, hitchkick, and landing. I bought videos and attended track coaching workshops. There were drills for everything. Jeff lifted weights, did plyometrics, and hurdled. I envisioned him as a contender for a state championship in our small-school classification, as a freshman. By the end of the year I had laboriously, painstakingly, in a detail-oriented, and supportive way coached a great natural long jumper all the way up to 17 feet 6 inches....

Coaching and teaching have much in common. The way coaches and teachers motivate kids is similar. We take raw talent and try and find a strategy and communication technique that will transmit a skill in an efficient manner so that success is achieved by the learner (and also by the teacher). Coaching was more important to me than teaching, in the beginning, because everything about sports is so out in the open, and it's fun to be around energetic kids committed to progress. Success, failure, highs, and lows are fairly easy to measure in athletics. Classroom successes sometimes seem arbitrary and difficult to measure. But, as time has passed, experience has taught me that success in athletics is shallow, fleeting, and rarely satisfying for long. As time passed, teaching increasingly captivated my mind, and I've become committed to and absorbed by it, hoping that its results will hold a higher level of significance and something of a greater and lasting value for my students.

This re-dedication to teaching encouraged me to be introspective and analyze variables that impact the teaching profession. One realization has been that as the years have gone by, many changes in educational theory and practice have occurred and been implemented in the schools where I have taught, usually as a part of a school improvement process, or to be innovative. Most of the ideas were repackaged theories with new terminology, with not much new substance, really. Most teachers, especially us old timers, were "grounded" in educational theories from people like Piaget, Maslow, and others. We wrote objectives, lesson plans, and unit plans, and then were introduced to wonderful new ideas like the "Hunter Model," Mastery Learning, Effective Schools, Left brain-Right brain, Teaching Styles, Critical Thinking, Cooperative Learning, Assessment, "Rigor and Relevance," PLCs ... and the list goes on and on, as it should.

Most of these ideas were presented to us through in-services and workshops organized by well-meaning administrators who had learned about them at an inspiring conference of one sort or another. One day it occurred to me that maybe my administrators were doing the same thing I had done with Jeff. With good intentions, they learned everything possible about good teaching and then came back to "coach" us. Trying to be a team player, I have gotten excited about some of these "new" concepts and included them in the things I do in the classroom.

I write the day's objective on the board (sometimes I even write the "State Standard" as well), knowing that all the students are anticipating that, making sure they aren't short-changed in what they came there for that day. I deliver the material in the proper teacher way, incorporating all the best old and new approaches such as: "Me, We, Two, You," monitoring and adjusting the pace, incorporating cooperative learning, and having closure. I top it off with all kinds of assessments, and then reteach, tutor, and retest when necessary.

One year, after previously doing my best to be conspicuously silent when volunteers were asked for committees (I'm not sure if it was out of guilt or all those "collegial staredowns"), I volunteered to be on the "Teacher Evaluation" committee for our school district and was promptly chosen to be the chairman. I think I must have gone for coffee when the vote was taken. Our goal was to devise a streamlined, mostly "formative" evaluation process that was complete yet efficient to use. We began by studying the most current teaching research, trying to develop criteria for what good teachers do, and finally, we prescribed a measuring instrument for that criteria. The process took over a year to complete, and the new evaluation procedure was used in that district for about fifteen years. For the most part, administrators and faculty were happy with it. We were proud of our work and convinced that it would help the district, which it did.

Reflecting on the evaluation committee's work, I have often wondered (probably because of guilt complexes dating back to my youth) if a teacher could know all the information a teacher should know, exhibit all the criteria a good teacher should exhibit, but still be a poor teacher. Could a teacher "ace" the evaluation but "flunk" the classroom? Worse yet, I have wondered whether it would be possible to ruin a naturally-gifted, novice teacher by using the evaluation process. Could we take such people, full of life, ideas, and creativity, and fill their heads with all this good information, conform them to a specific evaluation process, and turn them into dull, average teachers just like I turned that 19-foot freshman long jumper into a 17-footer? Do we squeeze the creativity, motivation, and innate ability out of wonderfully gifted teachers by hovering over them, forcing them to fit the evaluation mold? I hope not. I hope that in the process of conforming teachers to specific criteria, we don't create "robotic" instructors who follow a set pattern for effective teaching so that they can score well on evaluations, please administrators, and keep their jobs. Wouldn't kids be even more bored than they are already, if they have to pass through a full day of school with teachers who are nearly identical in their teaching styles and routines?

A most critical concern should be whether this "canned teaching" approach can be satisfying to "The Natural." I doubt it. I wonder how many "state champion" teachers never made it to the finals because they had to change their style to fit some evaluation process or some new approach their school district adopted. I wonder how many of these teachers change professions because they were stifled, frustrated, or just plain bored.

Teacher appraisal and performance evaluation is critical to school and faculty improvement. It is very rewarding and worthwhile to use the evaluation process to help teachers improve, become confident and effective, and, better still, to be allowed some flexibility in giving the "naturals" some space.

I learned a lot that first year of coaching track. Later on I had great long jumpers. I rarely coached them, I left them alone. One time another coach asked me what I did every year to get my jumpers to compete so well at the state championships. I said, "Nothing."

I had this twinkle in my eye and strut in my walk that challenged him not to believe me. But I was telling the truth.

.... 3 ....

Finding Martians
in the Dark

*S*hhh! *Bend over. Hold your breath. Here he comes around the corner. Crunch, crunch, crunch. I can hear him breathing. He's whispering to himself. What's he saying?*

"Where is that guy? He always hides down here somewhere. It's sooo dark I can't believe he'd stay here without getting scared."

I was hiding under the neighbor's evergreen hedge. My knees were scrunched up into my chest. I was leaning against a branch, motionless, and very quiet. It was very dark, plenty dark enough for me to be scared, but this was too important, and fear is put aside in crucial situations for a twelve-year-old boy.

My neighborhood friends and I were playing "Martian." A sophisticated game of hide-and-seek, it involved a person who was "it" and several who went to hide. When the person who was "it" found a hidden person, that person would help find the others. This would continue until everyone was found. A great game. It was best to play it in the pitch black dark. We used the whole block as the boundaries.

I'm not sure how old Mrs. Gutterman felt about having "Martians" hiding in her hedge at 9:30 at night in the summertime, nor was I ever quite sure what my parents meant when they said, "The neighbors are calling and complaining that you're making too much noise out there." After all, how could I be making too much noise with my knees drawn up to my chest while trying to not breathe too loudly? Neighbors sure have good ears sometimes.

My younger brother, Paul, and I were expert "Martian" players. We had a couple of places where no one could ever find us. My favorite places were on the back porch roof and under the hedge.

The roof was a great place. I would shimmy up the pillar and swing my right leg up and then sort of roll up onto the roof, kind of like getting out of a swimming pool. There were only two ways to see me up there. One was to climb up the hill in the neighbor's yard and look across and see me, which was difficult in the dark. The other way, of course, was to climb up and see me there, but all my friends were afraid of heights, so I was safe. Actually, I was afraid of heights myself, so the hedge was a much more attractive place to hide. I was encouraged to be afraid of heights by my mother, who would have had to patch me up if I had fallen fourteen feet from the edge of the roof down to the roof of the garage.

I never knew where Paul hid. We agreed to keep our places secret, and he has to this very day. It's been more than forty years now, and family picnics go amicably until I bring up the subject of his hiding place, and he mysteriously disappears with his family. "Martian" was a very important game and its effect on later life can't be overestimated.

Perhaps it was "Martian" that instilled in me an affection for hedges. I like all kinds of hedges: short, tall, coniferous, deciduous. In addition to the hedge I hid under, there was a neighbor across the street, Mr. Evans, who had a ten-foot hedge around his mansion. We could just barely see the top of the thirty room, four-story house. The mystery associated with that particular hedge and house added a lot of excitement to my life, very similar to the goosebumps I felt listening to ghost stories around a campfire. I couldn't believe it one day when Paul came home and told me he had slithered under the hedge and watched old Mr. Evans reading in the back yard. Paul had just moved up a notch on the macho scale. Hedges have a way of affecting your social standing.

I suppose it was not by accident that when I looked for a house to buy, I was attracted to one that had a hedge around it. Never mind that the house was falling apart and that the water was unpalatable. "Please, honey, not this one. It'll cost more to fix up than it will to buy," my wife begged. "But it has a hedge. I'll take it," I told the realtor. "You won't be sorry," the realtor said with a fiendish smile. I wasn't. I had bought a beautiful hedge and a six-bedroom house came with it as a bonus.

Then tragedy struck. My family and I went back to New England one summer. We made arrangements for a live-in housekeeper to take care of our black lab and the yard. In Wyoming's dry climate, this requires frequent watering and mowing of the lawn. When we returned in late August, we hadn't realized until then that asking a person for lawn and animal care in return for a rent-free six bed-room house (with a beautiful hedge) was unrealistic. Our lawn was brown, the VCR was ruined, there were several animal waste by-products in one of the bedrooms, and the hedge had been trimmed by someone who must have spent several years on a war ship. It looked like the ocean rolling at high tide.

We were very disappointed but didn't know the real effect on the hedge until the next spring. That year, when spring finally made it to Wyoming (July), I was expecting to straighten out the curves on the top of the hedge by invoking my expert pruning techniques. As I watched the grass and flowers take off on their spring growth, I was distraught to find that the hedge didn't fol-low suit. It must have died of stress caused by lack of water dur-ing the summer, which was followed by a long, cold winter. Most of the hedge was nothing but brown, scraggly branches with nothing on them, kind of like very skinny, witch-like fingers with no flesh.

It was ugly. I didn't know what to do about it. I decided to wait. Maybe it would bloom late. It didn't. I was just getting ready to dig the whole thing out of there and replace it with a white board fence when a wealth of lush, new green (hedge-type?) leaves began appearing around the base of the old hedge. I was relieved and excited. It looked like the hedge would save itself. I was glad.

27

My friend, Chad Wills, told me that "anybody who puts a board outside and paints it is out of their mind." (I wasn't sure what he meant, but I inferred that he meant that I would have to repaint a white board fence every year or two, interrupting my summer job of eliminating fish on the Powder River.) Waiting for the hedge to heal itself seemed like an appropriate thing to do.

The next major decision of the summer revolved around what to do with all the dead branches in the hedge. Should they be left to support and direct the new younger growth and then pruned out, or should they be pruned out all together right away, leaving the new growth free to grow in any direction? Being the hardworking yard type that I am, I decided to stay on the couch, leave the hedge alone, and see how fast it would grow back with the dead branches still in there.

A couple of weeks later, I noticed that my neighbor's hedge had grown what seemed to be a couple of feet already, and the new green growth in my hedge had barely risen a couple of inches through the tangle of dead branches. In a fit of energy and passion, I pruned out all the dead branches. A couple of days later, I looked forlornly at what used to be a very nice hedge and now looked like a reverse Mohawk haircut in various places, kind of like the time when my mom left the electric haircutter near me and went to answer the phone. I thought I would update hair fashion for six-year-old boys. There were huge holes in the hedge, with growth visible only inches above the ground. In other places the hedge was forty inches high with a nice flat, green top, just like it should be, but with large spaces interspersed throughout even this green mass. It was still ugly, but there was hope.

I had decided to leave a small part of the hedge untouched as sort of a control group to discover if I had made the right choice. This would allow me to become sort of a hedge "expert," and surely my friends and neighbors would then line up to ask my advice about hedge-raising, especially after they had observed this scientific method of data collection.

Within a couple of months of pruning out the dead branches, I had seen great growth in those areas. I realized that the dead branches were preventing and slowing the growth of the newer, green ones.

This initiated a fit of rumination over what had happened to the hedge over the course of the last couple of years, why the hedge was still so important to me, and what implications these things might have in relation to my own life.

First, the hedge was very important for more than just aesthetics. It provided shade for my dog to keep cool on hot summer days, and protection from predators for all the bugs, moths, and birds that called my hedge their home. It provided food for all kinds of creatures--berries for birds, leaves for all kinds of crawly things to hide in, and shaded, moist soil for worms and such. But a hedge has both limits and needs. It can only give so much, and it has to have water and nourishment from the soil.

People who are in leadership positions are sometimes like the hedge. They give and give and they protect. And others take and take and take until the leader dries up inside, a condition often called "burnout." This person needs water, a little space, and times of replenishment, to fill up until he or she is once again strong enough to nourish the others. I feel sorry for leaders who refuse to recognize that they are empty and need a break to refill. I also feel sorry for the takers because they usually have little empathy for an empty leader. They just run off to take from someone else until they dry them up, too.

It's in our own best interest to realize what good leaders do for us, how they build and inspire and protect us. Since good leaders are so rare, we should be sensitive to those times when they are drying up and help nurture them back to life.

The most important lesson of my hedge, though, related to its dead branches. They were stealing light and trying to steal nutrients from the new, growing branches that were so alive, vibrant, and refreshing. Isn't that the way it often goes? How many faculty meetings have we been to when some burned out, "dead" teacher voiced some negative and demoralizing opinion, and we could just watch a little air slip out of a beginner's vibrant balloon? Don't people who never have anything positive to contribute stunt the growth of the rest of us? The dead branches of that beautiful hedge were doing nothing positive for the rest of it.

Let us not deceive ourselves by thinking that teachers and administrators who have not "grown" in a long time can contribute much to a lively, enthusiastic, growing group. Unfortunately, they can steal light and sap life from the rest, eventually stunting the growth of the entire group, which in the long run negatively affects what the group can offer the kids entrusted to them. Students need to see enthusiasm and feel energy, following role models into discovery of many new things, making their lives much more positive and productive.

I feel sorry (actually, guilty is a better word, because I have done it myself) that some people feel compelled to express their negativity in meetings. Most of the time what they say is a thinly disguised attempt to avoid doing more, when doing more and better should always be evaluated in the framework of students' best interests.

I would much rather hear an excited, impassioned, verbal mistake from a glowing and growing, motivated teacher than all the wisdom in the world from a "dying" teacher or administrator.

I have to admit that I am sometimes like the growing part of the hedge, and other times I'm like the dead branches that do nothing but impair the growth of the rest. I hope that I can learn to keep my mouth shut when I am like the latter and open it when I am like the former.

After I pruned my Wyoming hedge, it grew much better and faster. I could hold my head up when I drove out of the driveway. I didn't have to put up a white picket fence. I could go fishing instead. My dog liked its shade, and the birds and moths (and most likely, the earthworms) came back. And occasionally, if I listened really hard, I could hear "You're it" in the back yard on those really pitch black nights. Some things never change.

········ *4* ········

Jargonasaurus I

Over the course of my long and arduous career I have seen many new teachers arrive on the scene, fresh out of college. These are usually bright, energetic, idealistic types of people who generally make experienced teachers nervous. Taking the responsibility on as an "extra-duty", we do our best to break them of these nasty habits and personality traits and fill them in on the "way things work around here". It doesn't take very long, depending on how hard we work at it, for them to mold with our ideas, and pretty soon everyone is comfortable again.

I often have wondered why these pretentious, energetic young scholars act the way they do. After many hours of introspection I decided that it is probably because of some "gap" in their undergraduate training. So I have taken it upon myself, once and for all, to guide young teachers in the appropriate behavior expected of all members of the teaching profession. This chapter specifically deals with the teacher (as opposed to textbook) "lingo", the vocabulary used in most school districts. After reading and studying this chapter, a new teacher should be able to effectively use teacher-type vocabulary around his peers with confidence, and in such a way that all will understand the nature of the conversation.

I am hereby going to the trouble of filling a necessary void in undergraduate teacher-education programs, offering this as my first installment of a teacher "Jargonasaurus", a partial list of words and phrases that includes most of my "favorite" misused terms:

"New Teacher"--This is a person who "volunteers" (and is expected to) for every unpaid extra-curricular activity and committee.

Everyone likes them and says, usually under their breath, "Go man go, we're all behind you. Let me know if you need any help."

"Tenure"--This is a point in a teacher's career when he ceases to volunteer for anything and is approaching something called "burnout", a term that will be discussed later.

"Tardy Bell"--This is a sound that only teachers can hear. Students claim that aging causes teachers to hear sounds like that. There will be many wasted minutes used in faculty meetings to discuss what the tardy bell really means and what to do about the "sound-challenged" students who can't detect it.

"Experience"--This characteristic allows teachers to know when and where food is going to be served at faculty functions so they can mysteriously appear at the front of the line at just the right moment. These people also seem to have a knack at getting out of the parking lot faster at the end of the workday.

"School Board"--(1) This is a group of people who usually say "yes" to ideas that don't cost anything and "no" to ideas that do. (2) A group of people who become experts on education after they get elected. (3) May include a member with a personal "axe to grind," which can make a lot of people "edgy."

"Objectivity and Understanding"--What parents usually have when a problem involves someone else's kid. A whole new level of depth of these two traits occurs when sports is involved. New teachers would gain a lot of both of these two traits if they could sit in on, and take notes, during meetings when coaches try to explain to parents why their child is not good enough to "start" on their team.

"Student-Teacher"--An in-school vacation plan for teachers.

"They only work nine months of the year"--This is a statement that seems to pop up around the time that contract negotiations begin every year.

"Standards-based Assessment"--Loss of class time to find out what students should be doing during class time.

"Test Scores"--These are important to a school district if the students score well, but a source of creative rationalizing for districts that don't.

"Curriculum"--This is the very important process of copying the table of contents out of a current textbook and wording it to look original. This can be an important source of dust should a new teacher need one. An important note here is that if new teachers are really good at using creative new terminology when they reword the table of contents they can sometimes be called "innovative".

"Inservice"--A vocabulary exercise for teachers. Although not as creative as the Jargonasaurus, teachers can learn important new terms during this exercise, especially the ones that rename things they already do. If teachers can invent new terms to be used in inservices, they might be able to earn a higher degree or act as a consultant, and make real money so they can afford to teach.

"Lunch Duty"--An exercise prescribed by administrators to help teachers continue to develop patience.

"Good Coach"--One who wins.

"Poor Coach"--One who develops character. This can also be a good coach who, one year won a championship, and mysteriously forgot everything he knew the next year, when the team didn't do so well.

"I don't get it"--This is a statement often made by students who weren't paying attention when you discussed a particular topic the first time. Occasionally it is made by students who missed school to go shopping or to the beach. It is your responsibility to reteach the subject since you obviously failed to make it clear the first time. You should also be required to evaluate the students' particular learning style, and adjust your delivery, so they can understand the subject better the second time around.

"Homework"--An ancient torture device used by teachers to ruin students' week nights and weekends. Teachers who love children would never dream of using such a cruel and unusual punishment as it might get in the way of the child's education.

"Good answer"--This is positive reinforcement given to a student whom you have chosen and primed to answer questions you ask while you're being observed by an evaluator. Careful consideration should be given to whom you choose for this task since you want to look good.

"Can I go to the bathroom?"--This is a question asked by students who either (a) haven't studied the functions of the human body, or (b) can't sit still any longer and want to aimlessly wander the halls while talking on their cell phones or texting their buddies who are wandering in a different hallway. Before giving permission, you should observe the student for the next few minutes. If he is a disruptive force in the class, it is obvious that he should get a pass to go to the restroom. In a more rare event, if his eyes appear to be floating, you should probably reply, "Yes, you may go to the bathroom," before you find out that he, in fact, can.

"Lesson Plans"--An obviously misguided attempt at predicting what will happen in your class. You will start out by covering sheets of paper with great ideas, and after a few years of experience you will be able to streamline them down to, say, one or two words. Don't forget to note which "state standard" you will be addressing in the lesson, and the adjustments you will make for special ed. kids, or you will be constantly running back to your file cabinet to make sure you didn't forget which ones they were.

"Merit Pay"--This is what you will receive if you agree with the principal all the time and take on more than your share of extra duties. Teachers who don't deserve merit pay think the criteria is ambiguous and subjective. When there is a limited amount of money to be doled out to meritorious teachers, it is an amazing coincidence how the number of teachers who evaluate at that level works out perfectly every time.

"Potential"--This refers to abilities that your "A" students have and what your poor students are obviously missing.

"Flexibility"--When you disagree with another teacher, this is a quality that they are missing and need to develop.

"Team Teaching"--This is when an inexperienced teacher gets to "work with" an experienced teacher and teach for a period, while the experienced teacher spends the time drinking coffee in the teachers' lounge.

"Class Clown"--This person has been added to your class list so that you may pay for sins committed earlier in your lifetime, particularly if you were one yourself. Guidance counselors are amazingly astute at knowing who deserves payback.

"Cooperative Learning"--A new and innovative trend in teaching technique that came out in the 1980s. Anytime now we will hear of a new variant of this technique which might be called "learning in groups", but we will have to wait and see.

Please consider this only a helpful and enlightening "first install-ment" of the Jargonasaurus, more of which is to come. By memo-rizing this terminology, a new teacher should be able to approach the teachers' lounge with the swagger of a ten year veteran. No longer does a rookie have to look bewildered and confused when discussing important basic educational issues with his or her col-leagues. It is my hope that I have been a catalyst in the school improvement process (a term in the next installment?), a process that has long been hindered by the misuse of educational jargon.

The Gardener

"And where do you live?" the carpet salesman inquired. I had just bought some carpet for my house, and he was planning on delivering it the next day. My wife and I were ecstatic, since we were now able, courtesy of the great American credit card, to get rid of our awesome shag rug. This would mean we could now have friends over without fear of imagining the sound of hysterical laughter as they were leaving. "We live on Adkins Valley Lane, about one mile south of the college, behind the large storage buildings."

How could he not picture a sophisticated place like that? I drew a small map on a piece of scrap paper. "Hey, is that the dirt road by the garden?" he asked.

"That's the one," I replied. "Just turn there and my house is the second one on the right." I was confident he knew exactly where to go.

A couple of weeks later we invited one of my teacher colleagues over for dinner. He asked where I lived, and a similar exchange of questions and directions was repeated. Once "the garden" was mentioned, the other directions were unnecessary.

As a matter of fact, any time I gave directions to my home, except for law enforcement, IRS agents, and other disreputable types, I just asked the person if they knew where "the garden" was, on the right about a mile past the college, and it was a cakewalk from there.

I did, however, miss diagramming the maps on napkins and such, while listeners rolled their eyes, trying to decipher my chicken scratchings. It's a good thing the garden was there, because once

I mentioned that, no one got lost trying to follow my excellent directions.

The garden was incredible, and its beauty and productiveness gave me many occasions for shallow thought. On the shallow end of things, I sometimes wondered how come I never worked that hard, or how come I could look at a bag of fertilizer, read it, and still not know how to spread it ... things like that. These thoughts didn't linger long as I didn't want to live with guilt over not knowing how to do anything practical or worthwhile with my hands. They say guilt causes lots of psychosomatic illnesses and I didn't want any of those, whatever they are.

On the deeper side of things, it came to mind that people tend to notice exceptionally excellent performance or exceptionally poor performance, remember it, and identify it with a place or person. Hardly anyone notices or remembers performance "in the middle," or mediocre.

The work of the gardener was his signature in the world. Everything he did affected the productiveness of his garden, and the results showed the value of his work. First, the design and setup of the garden showed that there was going to be an efficient use of water and sunlight. Each of the perfectly straight rows of plants had an irrigation line running to the head, and each line gradually sloped away so that the water would run slowly along each furrow and sort of die out right at the end. The eight-foot corn, the thousands of onions, and the bulging tomato plants, barely able to hold up the weight of the fruit, all were visible evidence of the gardener's care. They were planted in just the right areas of the garden so the taller plants wouldn't block out the sunlight from the shorter ones. Although very few people knew the gardener's name, everyone knew the gardener.

I lived on Adkins Valley Lane for a few summers, and only ran into the gardener a couple times. I often wondered how and when he got the work done on the garden with its perfectly straight, weed-free rows. I understood, when one day our track team had to leave for a track meet at 5:00 AM. I was driving down the lane in the gray of the dawn, shaking out the cobwebs of a lousy night's sleep, coffee in hand to keep it from spilling as I hit the potholes, and there was the gardener. He was a middle-aged man, maybe sixty years old, slightly overweight, wearing dark colored clothes and a sweater to ward off the chill. He was stooped over, spraying each individual onion plant with some sort of insecticide, or maybe it was "Miracle Grow." I wasn't sure.

I watched him in the side glow of the headlights as I drove by. I waved. He did not return my greeting. I couldn't help but marvel at his discipline, and I stopped my inward complaining about having to get up so early for the track meet. I wondered why I couldn't get up in the morning to jog or read as I had often resolved to do. That man certainly had something that I was missing, and it gave me something to think about.

The most amazing thing about the gardener was the harvest of the fruits of his labor. After all the work of the summer invested in that plot of ground: early mornings, irrigating, fertilizing, rototilling, composting of individual plants, weeding, pruning, and insect spraying, the gardener didn't pick any of it. That's right, none. We never saw him take a single vegetable or fruit from the garden. Oh, he allowed his relatives and friends to come over and pick his vegetables, and occasional neighbors (like me) might notice a few plants getting overripe and help themselves, but I never saw the gardener pick anything himself. I wondered how a person could put that much work into something and then not enjoy the successful results.

It dawned on me that teaching (and other people-serving professions) have a lot in common with that old gardener and his plot of ground. We do all the same things with human lives. We cultivate, protect, prune, and feed lives every day. We get to watch them grow and develop (for better most of the time and for worse some of the time), and just like the gardener, we rarely get to see the finished product.

Many of my former students have taken the fundamental science I have taught them and moved on to bigger and greater things than I ever thought of doing. They are my signature. There are also those students who were "lost souls" who, because of some teacher's love, interest, and role-modeling, amounted to far more than they ever could have imagined. They are our signature.

I learned a lot from the gardener. Although our occupations differed on the surface, we had much in common. I hope my signature is as easy to read as his. I have learned that, for the most part, success comes in many packages, and that the definition of success varies by individual--sometimes shallow, sometimes deep. For me, the depth of success and the meaning of it are intertwined, and I choose to take the depth from the value of the "journey," the effort and the commitment to the long ride of our profession.

Teaching is a beautiful occupation. It's a marathon, not a sprint, that includes a potpourri of successes and failures, times of creativity and boredom, times of frustration, anger and exhilaration, positivity and negativity. None of these stick out more than the others, but taken in total, with the effort involved, knowing that I did everything I could, that is what makes it good for me.

.... 6 ....

Swimming

"Oh, hello Mr. Biebel. Glad you could join us." It was the voice of my principal, Harriet Snowdon. "Sorry you were late for this faculty meeting," she said, "but we are glad you are here. Congratulations, you were just elected chairman of the Student Tardy and Absence Committee."

I sat down, looking forlorn, feeling victimized because my propensity to being tardy to meetings had once again been rewarded with such a high ranking position.

Sitting there sulking and listening with one ear, I realized that we were being informed about the progress of salary negotiations. Since it was March, it was predictable that the next few words would be, "The budget is tighter than normal this year," and "Insurance rates are going up, as you know." Ho- hum.......

We moved on to the next agenda item, which was to encourage input as to what classes everyone was going to be offering in the fall of the next school year as we needed to get ready for student scheduling. Somehow the discussion deteriorated when Hal Shorter raised the important issue of, "Why do we teach what we do anyway? Hardly any of it is usable, most of it is irrelevant, and the kids can't relate to it."

It's important to note that Hal was one of our very good vocational teachers, whose classes had seen a decline in enrollment. Additionally, the state and district had recently been "trendy" in decreasing their support for vocational education, while putting more emphasis on "college bound" types of classes.

Hal was one of my best friends, with a very practical outlook on

41

things, so shouldn't be taken very seriously. Meanwhile, having heard this conversation many times before, I didn't feel the need to defend the atomic theory, Einstein's theory of relativity, or any other irrelevant topics, most of which I teach. I was still remorseful for my evil tardy ways, or more precisely, I was especially remorseful for my new chairmanship.

As the discussion of the value of different subject matter raged forward, I began responding in my usual way. I drifted off to a distant place. I had been to many distant places during meetings, but this time I drifted off to a rustic cabin that my parents had owned during my childhood. Now, rustic today is not the same as rustic was in 1960. It meant the cabin was perfect, devoid of most creature comforts we have today, such as running water, indoor latrine, furnace, insulation, gas or electric stove, hot water. Like I said, it was perfect. It was a white one bedroom cabin, about 600 square feet, with an indoor wood stove that also served as a cooking stove. It had bumpy road access, and across the road on the west side was what a boy really needs: woods. Woods to hide in, cut down trees, make forts and tree houses, dig for worms and bury fish--there were all kinds of things to do. On the other side of the cabin, facing east, was the best part: Baptist Pond. A mile long and half mile wide, this New Hampshire pond had an island out in the middle and nice clean water for fishing and swimming in. It was heaven on earth for this eight-year-old boy.

I have been guilty of drifting off to this place in all kinds of meetings. In fact, I think once during church, my father, the pastor, stopped his sermon and asked me to come back from the pond, which is surprising since I was sitting in the pew right in front of him. Maybe he had drifted off there himself during his own sermon, which wouldn't surprise me, since he loved it there too.

My two brothers and my Dad were into boats and fishing. My Dad particularly liked to buy wooden rowboats with cracks in the floor that you could see right through when we first went to the cabin to launch them in late spring. We would paint the boats,

42

rebuild and paint the dock, clear and burn leaves and brush, fix the outside, and weatherproof the cabin. When we launched the boats, the water filled them up as they slowly sank into the pond. Dad said the wood in the floor would swell, then we would bail them out and they would be fine after that. This was one of my very first science lessons, and to my great relief, my Dad was very smart. The boats floated, and we had a blast growing up on that pond during the summers.

On the negative side, Dad had what I considered to be a character flaw: specifically, he was an extremely hard worker, always improving wherever and whatever condition we were living in, while of course providing us kids an opportunity to help. After a year or two the cabin had an addition or two, and we had increased our local stature.

We were able to help the neighbors with their decisions on whether they might want to sell their property on the pond when we progressed from boats with oars to boats with motors. My Dad liked old motors as much as he liked old rowboats. He must have, as he was always trying to figure out how to start them, which involved pulling on a rope with a knot at the end at least twenty-five times while pushing and/or pulling on a couple of buttons on the motor and sometimes squeezing on the black bulb coming from the gas tank.

Occasionally I got to hear some creative use of the English language, and some word combinations that I knew would benefit me later when I was big enough to pull on the cord.

"Hey Daddy, let me try. It's my turn."

"Shurfut, findingle, inglemittit, dawg ... haven't you got something better to do? Now go get that whachamadingy thing in the shed. It's right next to the thingamabob."

I have to hand it to my Dad. I never ever heard him say a cussword. His three sons, and this is not a confession or accusation of any sort, may not have been saddled with that particular weakness, or with the aforementioned "hard worker" character flaw, either.

As I mentioned previously, it was my brothers and Dad who were into boats and fishing. One day my older brother, Dave, came back from a hard morning's fishing with the whole bottom of the boat filled with perch, dead perch. I was so proud of him that I went in the cabin, where everyone else was just finishing breakfast, to brag for him.

"How did ya catch all those fish, and what were you using for bait, and where were ya catching them?" I asked.

"Those are all 'trade secrets,'" he whispered. "Real men don't tell stuff like that."

I was impressed to know "man" stuff at such a young age, and, when he saw that I was looking up at him with the devotion only a younger brother can offer, he said, "Now I'm gonna let you in on another secret, but you have to keep it between us."

"Ok, Ok, what is it?" I asked.

He said, "You know that hole you dug up in the woods yesterday, practicing for the future?"

"Yeah ... Yeah," I replied.

"Well, these fish here in the boat, they are supposed to be buried in that hole. Think you can do it and keep it a secret?"

"Sure. No one will ever know; it's our secret. Do we have to slit our hands and mix blood or something?"

"No, we don't have to be blood brothers. We're real ones, stupid."

I, myself, was different from my brothers and Dad because I would rather be swimming than fishing. So while they were off, pulling the cord on the motor and filling the boats with fish, I spent most of my afternoons swimming on the little beach we had put in, by hand, in front of the cabin.

I loved swimming. I took all the Red Cross swimming lessons at our town pool, moving quickly up through all the levels: beginner, advanced beginner, intermediate, and so on. But when I was at "the cottage," which is what we sophisticatedly called the cabin, I would be found diving down to find white rocks on the bottom and coming back up, sometimes yelling to Mom, "Mom, Mom, can you

44

come out and throw the rocks for me? Hey, watch this!"

Then Mom would get excited enough to get up off her chaise lounge, where she had been sunning herself, to throw rocks out in the water so I could find them.

"Hey Mom, how 'bout something else like a nickel or a quarter?"

It was hard for Mom to get anything done around the cottage, and I'm sure she would have preferred that I take up fishing. But she was a good thrower, although sometimes she would make a mistake and throw it out too deep and I would be really busy for awhile trying to find it. From time to time, I suggested that she work on her technique, offering to play catch with a baseball with her, but she declined. I think she said that she needed a little space, which I took to mean the kitchen needed to be cleaned up. So, afraid that I might be invited to join the fun, I let the conversation drop.

All that swimming was beneficial to me later in life, as I trained to become a Red Cross Certified Water Safety Instructor, which means I could be a life guard and teach swimming lessons, thus avoiding real work during the summers when I was in high school and college. I taught a lot of kids to swim, but the group that stands out, by a long shot, was the Shelburn Family, which had four girls: Sara, Donna, Millie, Becky, and one son, the youngest, Freddie. They came to take swimming lessons every day for about a month, with their mother Billie, to the camp where I lifeguarded in the afternoon and gave private swimming lessons in the morning. Starting with the simplest of skills, getting the face wet, and then going completely under, on to bobbing, standing in the water, face in and turning it to the side to breathe and then back in the water, blowing bubbles, prone floating, back floating, and kicking. All four girls moved through the traditional Red Cross program from skill to skill, most basic on up through all the strokes and kicks. In a very short time they were swimming around in the pond like fish--it was very rewarding. While the girls were taking lessons, Billie would sit there with little Freddie, watching and enjoying the girls learn and giggle. It was all great fun.

After the third week or so of watching the girls progress so fast and having so much fun, Billie decided it was time to get Freddie involved. "Do you think Freddie is too young to learn to swim?" she asked me.

"No, Freddie isn't too young," I replied. "But is he afraid of the water?" I asked this because the first step in deciding whether anyone can learn to swim is whether or not they can stand getting their face wet. I had seen Freddie playing on the beach and in the shallow part of the water, but never had I seen him actually put his head under.

"Let me see," Billie said.

"FREDDIE!" she called. "Come down here to the water."

Freddie reluctantly meandered down to join us, standing in knee-deep water. It was clear that he was aware of what we were discussing. "Dan wants to see if you will get your face wet, so we can get you started on lessons and learn to swim like your sisters. So go ahead and jump up and down and go under."

Well, I had never heard such a wailing, 'cept maybe when I dragged my cousin Ruth Ann up the stairs by her hair when I was babysitting one night and it was time for going to bed and she was dithering. One shouldn't dither. It has consequences. This is a lesson that Freddie learned rather abruptly when his mother (did I mention she was large) picked him up and dunked him under, not once mind you, but two or three times just for good measure.

Freddie came up sputtering and screaming and then took off back to his seat. "Do you think he's ready now?" she asked. I shrugged and left it open that we would see what might happen tomorrow. Well, the next day, Freddie, after much soul searching, and probably some more refined, overnight parenting from Billie, was ready. Holding his mother's hands, he went under a couple of times, thenwent on his own, then swam through my legs. He was ready. In a week, Freddie was swimming out to the "float." What a victory for him.

The Red Cross way of teaching swimming has worked for millions of people. You start by teaching basic, simple skills, and then progress to more complex skills. It has proven to be a highly successful way of drownproofing America.

It seems to me that teaching mental concepts should follow a similar approach--that we would teach about atoms before we teach bonding, and that would come before formulas, and a few years later we have a pharmacist or a doctor. It is my job to get students to the position where they have the option to continue to that kind of level, although if you took a snapshot of any particular school day it might be hard to see what the relevance of the particular daily subject matter is, just like it is hard to see how "bobbing" can contribute to a great swimming stroke.

My friend Hal's approach to teaching was "tunnel-visioned," appropriate for a school that was training young people for technical/vocational job skills, but not for others who might be future scientists/doctors/vets, etc. The best schools offer both, a balanced-approach, including all the options possible.

In Hal's defense, it is true that most students are not headed for college and probably shouldn't be. The removal of the vocational/technical programs from high schools is a serious mistake, with the consequence of increased dropouts, a low-skilled labor force, and too many unemployed young people on the streets with nothing to do and not much hope.

Crime anyone?

There is so much pressure on schools because of the testing and accountability of the "No Child Left Behind Act," that vocational programs have taken a serious hit because a lot of those students have trouble reading and need to use extra time for remediation.

Those people with the power to write statewide tests and determine curriculum need to be a little less "tunnel-visioned" as well. "Raising the bar" has some serious, unintended, negative economic and social consequences, and the effects of implementation should include a more balanced analysis of what will happen to those who don't survive these innovative ideas. A pretty safe prediction is that the result of this testing approach will be a higher dropout rate and lower scores for upper level students, as schools are forced to focus on raising the scores of their lowest 25 percent of students to reach their annual Adequate Yearly Progress (AYP) and get a passing school grade. A lot of students drop out because they realize that they can't pass the required tests, and the upper level students have time, lots of time, taken out of classes to prepare for the tests, thus losing curricular instructional time. Some parents, who can afford it, have adapted to this by taking their kids out of public school, either homeschooling them or sending them to a private school, which has the unintended effect of lowering a school's AYP and school grade because some of the better students have been removed and the mean score is lowered.

I believe that one of the next great steps that America will take will be that, at the tenth grade level, some students will test themselves out of a traditional school setting and into alternative vocational schools, not as a punishment but to give them a chance to learn a job skill.

"Mr. Biebel," the principal called me back to the moment. Sorry to come back, I nodded.

"It's time to go to first period."

I looked around, noticing that I was alone.

"OK. But do you have a white rock that you could throw over there--or maybe even a quarter or a nickel--so I could dive down and find it?"

.... 7 ....

Understanding Christmas

A round December first every year I start to panic when I realize that it's that time again, to buy Christmas presents for all those on the list. As usual, there are more presents to buy than there is money, so the season can be depressing. Handling holiday depression comes easy for me and takes a similar sequence of phases from year to year. Recognizing these patterns is the first step in a sort of "Christmas Therapy," so I thought I'd offer my help to those readers who have problems dealing with the holiday blues.

First is the Denial Phase. I openly deny that it is Christmas again. I have heard that if you believe anything hard enough it makes it true, which allows me to spend extra money on important things like new outdoor gear and related paraphernalia to fill up those empty spaces in my garage. I also hide all Christmas CDs, videos, books, and threaten to burn the Christmas decorations before the wife and children can find them.

One year I wrote a letter to the SPCCT (the Society for the Prevention of Cruelty to Christmas Trees) hoping that they could do something about the indiscriminate cutting of evergreens. This phase doesn't last long, however, as more than one day without cooked food can change a person's phase in a hurry.

The second phase is called the "Real Meaning of Christmas" Phase. My wife and I decide together that this year we will hold down the spending and concentrate on what the real meaning of Christmas is and what the first Christmas meant to all mankind. We decide that we will share these convictions with the children. We also know that the sincerity of our convictions is proportional to our debt load. This phase usually ends about two days before Christmas when a terrible guilt complex overtakes me. I get the feeling that concentrating on the real meaning of Christmas is like putting coal in my children's stockings. The third phase is about to begin.

The third phase is the Credit Card Phase. It starts out as a mild, "We'll just get the kids a few little things so that they can remember this Christmas," and ends up as, "I've got some of the greatest kids in the world so let's max out this card and worry about it later." This is the final phase of the Christmas Syndrome. Certain things that may come later, including suicide threats, bill collectors, and creditor phone calls should not be confused as being related to the Christmas Syndrome.

This year, though, I decided to go into business for myself in the hopes of raising some money to afford Christmas and avoid the Christmas Syndrome. I thought I'd market several ideas for Christmas presents for teachers to give their favorite administrator. These gifts would be ideal for any administrator, especially the more experienced ones, as they would understand the full meaning and necessity for them. Less experienced administrators would need help with the written instructions that come with the gifts, as they are written in the same format as other catalog gifts and the same number of parts are missing.

The first gift selection we offer is the Objectivity Detector, or OD. This is a miniature computer that can fit in the administrator's shirt pocket. A tiny wire runs from the computer to a lightweight, ear-shaped sensing device that can be clipped under the user's collar or lapel. The sensing device has a small disk-shaped piece of baloney clipped to it and held there by a release mechanism. When a teacher, student, parent, or board member comes to the office wanting something, the OD immediately senses whether the intruder is being objective or if they have some other self-interest in mind. If the OD detects the latter, it emits a sound that only administrators can hear (we know they hear things), the release mechanism is stimulated, and the baloney is thrown at the intruder. Other projectiles could be used to replace the baloney if the administrator is having a particularly bad day. The OD would be invaluable to the administrator, but discretion should be used as to when and where to wear it. Teachers' lounges and sporting events are good examples of places not to wear it, as the OD wears out quickly and baloney refills are hard to come by. The cost is a mere $79.50.

The second gift selection is an Automatic Coin Flipper. This invention is primarily made for those people who have to make tough decisions and occasionally struggle to do so. Several coins are available with the coin flipper. Our simplest model has a "yes" on one side and a "no" on the other. This one comes in black and white only and hasn't been used much in the last couple of decades, especially by the politically inclined.

Other models include one that has "decide yourself" on one side and "appoint a committee" on the other. One coin is blank on both sides so the administrator can fit the coin to the situation. One administrator used the following on the blank coin: "You've got to be kidding" on one side, and "Har,Har, Har" on the other. This illustrates the flexibility that this coin allows.

A fourth coin could be used around contract negotiation time and would have "gloom" on one side and "doom" on the other. One should hide this coin because it has been known to disappear from administrators' filing cabinets.

The third gift selection is a Stressometer. This object looks similar to a circular barometer, complete with a pointer. The pointer points to a scale that reads from 1 to 10. Low numbers represent low stress and high numbers represent high stress. The Stressometer should be strategically placed in the principal's office where people who enter it can see it immediately. If you enter the office and the Stressometer is showing a reading above 6, you would be wise to get the heck out of there and forget about what you wanted. In this way the Stressometer has proven to be a valuable tool for the health and safety of faculty members. Documented research, based on use of the Stressometer, shows that teachers should not even approach the principal's office on: the first day of school, the days before holidays, days of school board meetings, after fights with their spouse, and after parent conferences. A ten year warranty is available with this product since it has been known to blow up when the needle moves past 10. A new model is under construction and has a scale that reads from 10 to 25. This model would be appropriate for middle school principals (or teachers), and also administrators who work in large cities. The cost of the low budget Stressometer is a mere $82.50, unless you purchase the warranty which adds $2,500 to the cost because of the risk that this particular gift will wear out quickly due to overuse.

Our last selection offered this year is our "Talking Chair," which is a very comfortable chair to be placed in the principal's office and to be sat in by visitors to the principal such as students who are in trouble, teachers for evaluation conferences, and parents there to register complaints. The chair is outfitted with an internal "source-programmable" speaker in the back, near the head level. "Source-programmable" means that the administrator is able to program little messages that the person who sits in the chair will hear while they sit there.

This could be an extremely valuable way of communicating information to the person who is there to have a "one-on-one" with the principal--for example, to register their input/complaints. It could also allow principals a way of saying what they really want to say but can't because of the delicate nature of certain things that might need to be said.

Perhaps an example would clear up any confusion: Say Ralph Elsom, who is barely hanging on 'til retirement and hasn't done a single creative activity in his class for the last five years, is in for his year-end evaluation. The principal, resigned to the fact that there is nothing that can be done, says, "Well, there you go, Ralph. That covers it. It was good to have a sit-down and chat for a bit. Hope the family is good. Just sign on the bottom there and we'll be done."

Then the principal pushes a little button under the center portion of the desk, activating the speaker in the chair, which says in a computer monotone voice, "It's time to retire, Ralph, so we can get someone in here with a pulse."

It's very important to note that the principal must maintain extreme caution and not display any change in facial expression so Ralph thinks he is hearing things and decides he is getting too senile to teach any longer. As a result, Ralph might say, "You know, I think I'm going to hang it up this year. I've had enough." The principal replies, "I don't know how we'll ever get along without you, but come back and visit when you get a chance."

Suppose a parent comes in to complain about daughter Mary, who rarely makes it to school, is in trouble with the law, and has been suspended several times for being belligerent in class.

"Thank you for coming in, Mrs. Pleasant," the principal says. "Why don't you have a seat in this comfortable chair right here and tell me what your concerns are."

Then, while the parent is deriding anyone and everyone associated with the school for misunderstanding and mistreating her daughter, thus turning her into the victim that she obviously is, the principal listens and nods, emanating compassion. When the parent finishes and the decibel level lowers to a manageable level, the principal calmly replies, "I apologize for the mistreatment your beleaguered daughter has had to endure, and I promise you we will make every effort to improve our interaction with her so she can have every opportunity for success in the future."

The principal then pushes the button under the desk, the phone buzzes (this option costs extra), and the principal says, "Please excuse me. This will only take a second."

As the principal is mumbling quietly into the phone to no one, the chair continues the former conversation with something like, "But it will be a miracle if your daughter doesn't end up in jail, and it's mostly because of what you are doing right now, backing her up, when she needs to be held accountable. Why don't you go home and act like a parent should?"

While the parent is looking wildly around for the source of the voice, it is paramount that the principal continue mumbling into the phone, oblivious to the conversation between the chair and the parent. The parent, as a result, becomes bewildered, incoherent, and unsure. Thus, when the principal hangs up the phone and says, "Is there anything else I can help you with, Mrs. Pleasant?" The parent declines and quickly leaves the office.

One can see that the real value in this gift is the flexibility of situations it could be useful for. Of course, the "programmable" part will require a great amount of expertise, so we suggest you bring in someone from far outside the district to program the chair, as things like this can start rumors when a local person starts putting buttons under desks and such. Also, the circle of people who know about the chair has to be limited to, say, one principal from outside the district, who may need your help and support from time to time. The cost of this chair is $1,862.54, but one has to remember that it is still in the research and development stage.

One other thing to remember is that this chair has a long warranty, and it is bound to last well into the administrator's retirement years, so it will inevitably end up at home. Certain in-home uses for this chair might include, for example, convincing uninvited solicitors to help me market the chair and my other gifts. It might also be helpful when the administrator's spouse is resisting some reasonable request such as the purchase of another fishing pole, a $50,000 bass boat, and a camper with which to pull the boat to the lake. The options are limited only by one's imagination. In fact, I think I just heard my own chair tell me it was time to watch figure skating.

So there you have it. The money I raise from these devices should help me afford Christmas and maybe avoid the Christmas syndrome. In addition, it will help those teachers who often have to make the difficult choice of what to get their favorite administrator for Christmas. Please send a cashier's check or money order. Credit cards are not accepted since yours, like mine, may still have issues from last Christmas.

8

The Custodian

Mike Miller is one of the favorite characters from my past. Mike and his wife, Susan, were the custodians of a small high school in north central Wyoming at which I was privileged to teach for five years. Mike and Susan were nearing retirement after serving the district for twenty-five years. They were in charge of maintaining the high school and the teacherages, one of which my family lived in.

Mike was proud of his work, opposed to most new ideas, very opinionated, and disdained most people in general. He was gruff, ornery, confrontational, and often expressed his views without being asked. His stature reminded me of my grandfather: short, a little rotund, and balding. He had false teeth that he liked to click back and forth somehow when he was getting ready to expound on something. He was almost always dressed in green or khaki work pants and shirt with a worn set of work boots.

His favorite pastime was waiting for the teachers to go to first period class so he could clean up the goodies people brought to the teachers' lounge to feast on. If you wanted to get something to eat, you needed to get it before first hour. I often wondered how there could be an entire chocolate cake available before first period and none before the beginning of second period, which just happened to be my planning time, when I was hoping to help it disappear.

Mike was also proud, and certainly not secretive, about his daily schedule, especially the fact that he arose at 4:30 every morning (difficult to document for the rest of us), walked to school, and got most of his work done before the rest of us had cleaned the seeds out of our eyes. "Mornin' Dan," he would say. "Nice sunrise this morning. Did you hear the birds singing?" He never failed to let us know what time the sunrise was and how good it would be for us to get in the habit of contemplating its value in our lives. I especially enjoyed how he liked to rototill his garden at 5:00 AM, since I was his neighbor.

The first run-in I had with Mike was when I started coaching junior high basketball. I was interested in starting a "feeder" program for the elementary schoolers, and was looking the tiny gymnasium over to see how we might be able to lower some of the baskets so the little kids could shoot the ball with greater success. Mike came sauntering into the gym and was giving me and the principal the evil eyeball as he wandered over to listen to our conversation.

"Whacha doin'?" he asked.

I said, "We're trying to figure out how to fix these baskets so we can lower them for the little kids and raise them back up for the big kids when we want." I had seen this in the YMCAs in the nearby bigger towns and was proud to be doing something so humanitarian for the kids in our little place.

"Whatya gonna do that for?" he asked. "They'll just tear the blankety blank rims down," he said. "Then you'll really be in a bind."

"I just want to do something for the kids that will help the basketball program," I countered, obviously having the higher ground in this discussion. In his tactful and well thought-out way, allowing room for my feelings, I'm sure, he said, "I don't care what you want, Dan. I been here a long time, and every time we do something for these kids they just tear it up and then Susan and I have to fix it."

I lost control for a second and said, "We can't stop doing things for kids just because you might have to fix things once in awhile."

That was a really dumb thing to say, because the next sentence was the last time Mike spoke to me for a couple of months. "Oh yeah," he said, "and you can sweep your own gym floor, and your classroom from now on. Don't expect no help from me."

I'll have to hand it to Mike. He was a man of his word. I was a busy little beaver for awhile after that, doing a few extra things around my room and the gym.

The lesson I learned right then is the most important thing that teachers should know before they start teaching. The most important people in your lives as long as you are a teacher are your students. The second most important person(s) in your life is/are not your administrator, school board, or parents. The hierarchy of control in a school building starts with the school secretary, and that person shares the responsibility with the custodian for running the school. The principal is only a figurehead after that.

I believe that there may be a little known, semi-secretive committee that meets every day, maybe even before school, composed mostly of people in khaki pants and work boots. These people control pretty much everything that matters, and they are sometimes good about passing important tasty tidbits out to the community at large (or at small, depending on your community's size) about "what's going on down there at that school." After that one incident with Mike, I became one of the most highly qualified brownnoser teachers of all the secretaries and custodians I ever ran into. And, in case you're interested, I never did get those baskets adjusted.

I learned a lot more about Mike and Susan in the ensuing years. Their actions certainly belied what Mike showed on the surface. He and Susan treated that school building like it was a brand new Rolls Royce. It was easily the best kept building in town. They worked as hard as anyone could, primping and prodding, to highlight every sense of class and beauty that building could possibly render.

Kind of what I'm trying to get out of my students, I thought. I also learned that, underneath the ornery exterior was a heart of gold and a love for children. I found out that Mike and Susan didn't have to be doing this at all, since they owned land with oil wells in Texas, and could have easily lived off the royalty payments and been very comfortable. Somehow that increased my appreciation for them tenfold.

I didn't properly respect Mike's discerning capabilities until one day a couple of years after the basketball net discussion. We were having a very wet spring (in Wyoming that means snow in March that melts in May). When that happened, we inevitably were scourged with mud. Lots of mud. Not ordinary mud, but mud with bentonite in it. The hills there were loaded with it, and it was impossible to walk, drive, or do anything on dirt in those conditions. Mud with bentonite in it cakes onto shoes and sticks for days like super glue. It builds up and can turn a midget into a towering giant in a matter of a hundred steps or so. Whenever we got mud, Mike was bound to be in a bad mood. It was as predictable as a Road Runner cartoon--bee beep, bee beep, blam.

I was on my way into the building in the morning, and there was Mike, waiting to tell everyone to clean off their shoes so as not to track mud all over the carpet. He was pacing back and forth, talking to himself, teeth clicking away, and red-faced. Known to be a fast-learner, I took these as clear signs to keep my mouth shut.

"That blankety blank Reg Foster," he nearly yelled. "Look at what that bugger did. He had three inches of mud on his boots and didn't even think to wipe it off before he got in the building. Now look at the carpet. His dang father did the same thing eighteen years ago."

Now I got more interested. "You were here when Reg's father went to school here?" I asked. "Yeah, and the good for nothing SOB did the same thing," Mike replied.

I went to my room, after carefully removing my shoes, to avoid further discourse. I began to think about what Mike had said. In fact, I thought about it for several days. Actually, I have been thinking of it since then until now. At first, I kind of admired a man who could hold a grudge that long and even remember, to the year, how long it had been. I wondered how long it would take him to forget the little run-in we'd had in the gym two years earlier.

A second, deeper insight came to me after a long time of chewing on this muddy event. I had been fortunate to get to know Reg Foster, his father, grandmother, and the rest of his family and had become close friends with them, close enough to share a meal and shoot the breeze about pretty much everything from hunting, fishing, religion, politics, and even education. A lot of times, there was mud on the floor near the door.

It was clear that the family didn't value education to the same degree as other families did, and certainly not to the level a teacher would wish to see. These values threaded their way through the entire family, providing a framework for each generation just as clear as any physical, genetic trait. It was their culture, their tapestry, so to speak, and it would be the biggest obstacle for any teacher to overcome to get them to reach their "academic" potential, with such cultural resistance.

I had just learned something they don't teach in "teacher school," that if you are going to survive through thirty years of a career in this field, you have to accept that there are good people that you will come across who don't care much for and who don't value a "book-learnin," education the way that you do. Their kids go to school in every school, and sometimes the attitude is community wide. Sometimes they drop out. They don't respond to "teacher-methods" that work for "book-learnin" kids. If we want them to survive as book learnin' students, we're going to have to develop down-to-earth, practical connections for them to see why it's important.

Fortunately, at this school, there was an excellent vocational program for students like Reg, geared to help them learn to build and fix things. Reg Foster just wanted to drive heavy equipment. He's maybe forty-five years old now and that's what he does. He makes a good living and his own kids have the same motivations. As far as he is concerned, he's a success and he's happy. And he's not a loser because he didn't pass three years of math, and neither is the teacher. The world needs heavy equipment operators.

On the other hand, there has been occasion where teachers who are stimulating and creative have been able to provide students who come from a background such as this, but want to achieve more, a different lifestyle. These kids are rare and very special, as it takes great discipline to become a high achiever without home support. We are their only hope. No one else out there is able to be their advocate. No one. It's us or nobody. Let's remind them that they can do anything, be anything. Let's believe in them, guide them, and nourish their dreams.

I had learned that Mike and Susan liked to eat fish and that it was supposed to be a part of their diet. Since I liked the catching part, I took all the trout I caught over to their house and they enjoyed eating them. Those trout, plus my wife's monthly batch of chocolate chip cookies, eventually returned me to Mike's good graces, and we had a cordial relationship from then on.

Mike and Susan eventually retired and moved to Texas. I missed Mike. As long as I taught in that little town, I chuckled to myself when it got muddy in the spring, and I wished he was at the door to give me a bit of wisdom to chew on just like he had done in the old days.

········ 9 ········

Discipline and Other Fine Arts

"Hey Dan, can I see you a minute?" Mr. Rollins, the huge, booming-voiced, assistant football coach, biology teacher was talking to me in a serious sort of "you don't really have a choice here" tone, so I said, "Sure." A twist in my gut told me he wasn't going to ask me what I wanted for Christmas. I knew I had been tormenting his class for a couple of weeks.

So after the bell rang, I waited for him to say what was on his mind and was surprised that it took him so long to get to the point. "You've been tormenting my class for a couple of weeks now and I'm sick of it. Do you see what I have here in my hand?" Mr. Rollins held out what we called a "warning" which had all the little boxes under the "behavior" section checked off.

"What are you going to do with that?" I asked.

"It's Friday," he said, "and if your behavior doesn't improve by next Friday, I'm sending it home to your Dad."

Unaware that he knew of my Dad's lack of patience with unruly children, particularly his own, I meekly replied, "No problem, Mr. Rollins, you can rip it up right now if you want, cuz this class disruption is over."

"I hope so, but I'll hang on to it just in case you need a little incentive," he replied.

The weekend went by pretty fast. On Monday and for the rest of the following week I exhibited the youngest case of Alzheimer's disease ever known to exist. On Friday, Mr. Rollins approached me at the end of class and amazed me with his stern look and announcement that he had taken the liberty of using the postal service to pass the warning on to my father.

I wasn't very excited about what might lie ahead of me that evening as I saw my father as the fastest draw on the east coast, i.e., he could unhook, free, and deliver his belt to my rear end faster than a rattlesnake can strike. My brothers and I called him "Quick Draw" after one of my favorite cartoon characters. A Baptist preacher, with a stern idea of what proper behavior was, he passed those ideas on in sincere, fair, but often painful ways. He could look at my report card and see all A's and B's, except one low grade in "deportment," and I was in the doghouse for awhile. "But Dad," I would say, "if I get all those A's, shouldn't I be able to enjoy myself a little?" Whack! Once again I hadn't thought that one through ahead of time.

So I devised a plan. I figured that if I invited Fred Ruggles (my lab partner) home for the afternoon, my Dad wouldn't want to embarrass himself with one of those temper tantrums in front of Fred. Alas, when we got to the front door, my Dad was waiting inside with the warning in his hand, and the I-mean-business look on his face. He didn't realize I had Fred as my ace in the hole so I chuckled to myself.

"Who's that you got with you? Is that Fred?" he said. *Yep, good ol' Fred*, I thought. *Always there when you really needed him*, I snickered, to myself.

"Hey Fred," Dad said, "Dan's gonna get a whoopin. Do you want one, too?" I turned around to see what Fred had to say, and he had mysteriously disappeared, leaving me to face the impending doom by myself. This incident profoundly affected my life in several ways:

1. I learned that friendship is usually shallow and can be painful;
2. That I wasn't a very good strategist; and,
3. That I should become a teacher and become the giver rather than the givee, which leads me to the point of this important story.

Now that I have been a teacher for a long time, I realize that students fear several things that could happen to them at school. There's the "progress report," the phone call, the trip to the Principal's office (or the Dean's Office depending on the school), and the parent-teacher conference. Now that I have had school-aged kids of my own, I have come to fear these also. The purpose of this thesis (used loosely I'm sure), however, is to alleviate the fear most teachers feel when, either starting out as a new teacher, or starting out a new year of school, they wonder how they are going to handle discipline for students such as myself.

I would like to start off this discourse with a snappy saying like "The only thing we have to fear is fear itself," or "Fear is the product of ignorance," but I doubt if those would endear me to the reader too much. Having the necessary experience as a disruptive student in the past, however, gives me great credibility and expertise in this area, so teachers who read this will want to pay attention.

Over the years, I have seen other teachers develop and use effective discipline strategies that are simple and work for discipline problems. Mr. Rollins used an effective method on me. Mr. Martin, my ninth grade civics teacher, kept me home from a basketball game to teach me a lesson in consequences. But I hereby give the award for "most creative" to Miss Figgins, my eighth grade math teacher, who suggested to me privately that I was needing to move at a "faster pace than the rest of the class" (which I was unable to keep secret), so she moved me out into the hall with my desk to work "at my own pace." Not 'til I had a student similar to myself did I realize that "what goes around comes around," and that the real reason why I was out in the hall was so Miss Figgins could survive emotionally. It also dawned on me why my parents sent me to summer camp for long stretches of the summer year after year ... but that's a different story.

Here are some thoughts to help reduce your fear of having to discipline students, or the fear that you will not know how:

First, remember that the student, at least most students who are problems, do not have it "in" for you. The bigger picture is that it's not about you (the teacher). Not once in my years of tormenting teachers was it my design to intentionally ruin a teacher's day, hurt them, have them feel defeated, or even make it some sort of contest with the teacher. It was all about approval, and attention meant approval to me. I needed approval from everyone, especially my peers, but also adults.

It would take a hundred pages or so to try to give you a psychological perspective as to why I needed approval, and teachers do fall into that trap (trying to focus on the causes), or we can accept the fact that some students really do need approval and it causes a lot of their negative behaviors. It is also true that there will be other reasons why students act up. Remember, *it's not about you*, so try not to take it personally, and remain as detached as possible so you can be objective and focus on the solutions.

Second, remember that everything that happens at school should be part of a student's education. So when students get out of line, our role is to help them see that their behaviors are supposed to fit the particular social context they are in. Related to that, it is important that they learn to adjust behavior from teacher to teacher, as they will have to have this skill when they enter the real world. Several schools I have taught in have been a little too paranoid that every teacher be consistent, basically disciplining students the same way on everything, even making long and detailed lists of behaviors and corresponding consequences that students will be bringing on themselves when they screw up. This can be counterproductive as it removes the responsibility and accountability of behavior from the student and places it on the school. I know that schools need rules and levels of consequences, particularly for serious offenders, but I believe that students need to learn to adapt to having different expectations from different adult people who oversee them, just like it will be for them in the real world.

Here's an example of how to respond when a student gets out of line (disruptive), sleeps in class, has low grades, etc. I might say, "This is a really good thing that just happened, Sharon. Your behavior is keeping you and the rest of us from conducting class, so you get to learn that this kind of behavior manipulates me to act on it, which I now have to do because it's 'free' to learn it here."

Since some students, needing approval from anyone, usually equate that with the amount of attention they can get, it is silly to think that confronting them in front of their classmates will do anything but reinforce the opposite of what a teacher is trying to accomplish. This is why you (the teacher) should never get into a verbal exchange with a student in front of a group of his peers. He will get what he wanted all along and you will not accomplish what you would like--progress in class control.

I have had quite a few students with absence problems and some who attend but do no work while they are there. Keeping in mind the goal above, that everything students do or don't do in school should be a lesson, rather than getting all worked up over absences and apathy, getting in their face, or saying something I wish I hadn't, I have resolved to let them fail. I had a fun student, Marcus, who would come into class tardy almost every day, who often said, "Hey, Mr. B. How come I can do nothing in my other classes and get a 'C,' but I am failing in here?" He retook the class the following year, was on time, and worked hard enough to earn a "C," which was a big victory for both of us.

I spent my first fifteen years of teaching trying to prod, encourage, and get kids to change, with little success. Over the past fifteen years I have had a greater success rate with these students when I "failed them, with encouragement," which means that I had a conversation with them to remind them that they had earned an "F" because I loved them and wanted them to know that I thought they were smart enough to figure out what they needed to change to be successful. I have had far more students change for the better as a result of this approach. Failure, although painful, is a great lesson for students, especially if it is reinforced with guidance. Think about it, how many "teachable moments" have you had that came about by success and how many came about because you learned from a negative result?

You can also get good results by taking certain measures to proactively prevent negative behaviors:

Take advantage of the first two days of school to set out your behavioral expectations, and be as specific as possible. Do not threaten, but be serious, letting them know that the reason for the expectations is so that the class can run efficiently and learning can take place. Make sure they know that is the number one goal of your class, and that if what they do interferes with that goal, it will manipulate you to make something happen discipline-wise so that the class may return to maximum efficiency.

The first day of school will be a good time to show them you will be in control of the classroom. A simple way of doing that is to decide yourself where they will sit the very first day. Second, if a student presents you with an opportunity to assert discipline, don't miss it. This is a perfect opportunity to send a relatively benign message to the whole class of who will be in charge.

The first day of school is when a teacher should outline behavioral expectations, discipline steps, and consequences that occur if expectations are not met. For me, discipline steps are simple: non-verbal cue, verbal cue, adjust seat location, detention (sometimes rescinded if behavior is self-corrected), detention, referral, etc. This discussion would also include what will happen if students choose not to respond to the discipline action.

Suppose, for example, two students are talking while I am trying to teach. I say, "Would one of you move to an empty seat, please," and immediately return to the teaching. No confrontation. The consequence of inaction on their part was outlined on the first day of school, so they know what will happen if one of them doesn't move.

A more common preventative practice of good teaching is to establish procedures for doing the mundane things such as how to distribute and collect papers, how students will bring passes in, use the restroom, sharpen pencils, discuss personal issues with absences/assignments/grades, and other matters. These come up every day and in almost every class. The first two days of school good teachers will have resolved how they intend to handle these activities with very little loss of instructional time. A lot of behavioral issues start or get out of control during these "down times," while a teacher is inefficiently handling these duties.

The point is that the teacher should focus on teaching, showing that teaching/learning is the main event here, while negative responses will be addressed privately and after class. The first two days of school is a teacher's best opportunity to set the stage for acceptable behavior and common procedures to follow for the rest of the year. Too many teachers don't take advantage of their "captive audience" on the first day, trying to seem "nice and touchy-feely," and two months later can't figure out why it's such a struggle to be a teacher, since every day is misery for them.

The second most important thing you can do is to be a role-model of what you expect students to be. This means that you are serious about learning, you use time wisely--meaning that you start class right on time, that you teach or have learning activities for the whole class period (bell to bell), you keep grades up-to-date and posted as often as possible, and are generally efficient yourself. There are too many teachers who, after being tardy to class themselves, mark down students and discipline them for being tardy. Other teachers, adamant about student work being turned in on time, can sometimes take weeks to return students' graded work. You will have more credibility if you have the same standards for yourself as you do for your students.

Prevent negative things from happening by certain practices you do. One way you can keep students like me from getting out of control is to engage them early during the class period. When we are doing class work/practice work on some basic chemical calculation (I teach science), I use "extra credit" as an incentive to keep students involved in class. I might say something like, "Who can tell me the relationship of the volume of a gas to the pressure on it?" Johnny responds that it's "inverse," which is correct. I reward him by saying, "That's +1 for you." This gives him the attention and approval he's wanting and at least gets him off to a good start. He puts a +1 on the paper we're working on. I give +1, +2, or +3 for answers to problems, or good questions asked, and especially if they correct me for something I said or wrote on the board, and I thank them for correcting me for the mistake which, of course, I made on purpose.

When students turn in their work they have their extra credit added into their grade for the work. There are other ways to keep them involved, using competitions, timed activities, lab activities, and group work. The main thing is to find a technique that works and fits with your personality, philosophy, and style of teaching to keep them involved, and as soon as possible during each class session.

Don't be afraid to assert yourself when students participate in group activities. Set up groups so that continuously disruptive students are not in the same group together, and that the groups are spread out in such a way that these students are far apart. Do this early in the year. If, later, a couple of misbehaving buddies want to be in a group together, you could say something like, "Let's try it this time and see how it works out," and then use it as a learning/reinforcement tool both for them and for yourself, depending on the results.

Of course, if you are doing a group activity that involves a safety issue, design the activity ahead of time including: where you will position yourself, how materials will be dispersed, how cleanup will take place, spreading the groups out as much as possible. You should ask yourself, *What are potential problems that could happen during this activity?* and take steps to minimize them. Depending on the goal of the activity, you should model how students are to perform the different skills before they do them by themselves. You are just asking for trouble if you assign kids a group activity with only a set of directions.

Finally, remember that a lot of teachers at your school have been through what you are going through. They are the best resource beginning teachers have to help them with discipline, and will have great insight available with a particular group of kids, in this particular setting, and with the particular set of administrators and support they have to offer.

A few summers ago when I saw one of my former teachers, long retired Mrs. Peretti, I asked her, "Do you remember me?" She replied, "Well, now, how could I forget *you*?" I knew what she meant, and am embarrassed by it, but I have to say it is my former "life of crime" that helps me prevent the same in my current students.

········ *10* ········

The Brotherhood

When I was younger, I really loved to run. In the second grade I could run all the way home (about a half mile) without stopping at lunchtime. Sometimes I would run so that on each stride I landed on the crack that separated the sections of sidewalk. That was until I learned it would break my mother's back, and since fixing my own lunch didn't fit in with my busy elementary schedule, I quit the crack-landing habit. I don't remember ever running back to school after lunch, unless it was marble season.

When I got into the junior high, the goal was to run the mile-long loop which we called "the square," that circled the small Vermont town where I lived. Each week, I would see how long it would take to run the circle, which started under the big clock on the Congregational church. My goal was to do it in less than five minutes. Occasionally, I convinced a few of my friends that this would be good for them as well, but what I really wanted to do was to run them into the ground. There's nothing worse than a runner with an ego problem.

In high school I took a more disciplined and serious approach to running. The way I saw it was that I would do anything that needed to be done to ensure that I would cross the finish line first. I wasn't really interested in the other runners that much. I couldn't control what their goals were, although I'm sure my coach would say that I set a good example for them. If the other guys ran three miles, I would run five. If they ran ten 220s (we did "yards" in those days), then I would run an extra five. If I found out that a good runner on another school's team was running five miles, then I would run seven.

In college I took the same approach, only this time it was much more serious. It wasn't unusual for me to run over 100 miles in a week. One time I heard of some runners who were running 200 miles in a week, so I decided to try running more. The most I ever did was 140 miles in a week--eight miles in the morning and twelve at night, seven days a week, all alone. During one particular stretch of hard winter I hadn't done any speed training, so I snuck into a local high school and did forty repetitions of 220 yards in a long hallway they had there.

Needless to say, there wasn't much time or energy for other activities. I was an addict. Not much else really mattered to me. After college I continued running for a while. I still had the same childhood dream, that I would someday be able to stand on the award stand at the Olympics and have someone put the gold medal around my neck. I ran so many miles and competed in so many road races that the memories are only a myriad of mental pictures now. I did what most coaches want athletes to do: pay a price to reach a goal and leave the excess baggage aside.

After my running career was past, I took up jogging from time to time. This usually occurred after the holiday season when I noticed that my pants were getting tight, and I couldn't afford a new wardrobe since I had maxed out my credit cards on Christmas. The jogging phase went like this: A couple of weeks of a mile or two per day at an easy pace. Then a couple of weeks of a mile or two daily at a little faster pace, remembering that we're only doing this to lose weight. Then a couple of weeks of three miles daily, and so on.

After about a month, the desire to go out and race the other old-timers would return, and I would begin to get frisky and want to compete again. So I increased my mileage and began competing. When I lived in Wyoming, my favorite race was the Peaks to Prairie Triathlon. It starts in Red Lodge, Montana, and ends in Billings, Montana. I ran the first leg of three legs for a team. The leg was 8.8 miles. Each year it got longer (although the starting point and finish line remained the same).

My goals were different now: finishing and not embarrassing myself being the primary one.

One year, I learned a lesson while I was running in that triathlon. About the fourth mile I was beginning to "die." To a runner this means agony has just set in. It used to be fun, but now it hurts. My legs, which, until moments before, felt like they had wings attached, had just had a twenty pound weight attached at the ankle by some demon bystander around the four mile mark.

I struggled on. I thought about how far it was to the finish line and knew I didn't have a chance. I also thought about my team-mates and that our relationship was about to be strained. I began to rationalize this through, and decided that I didn't want to be friends with guys that did weird things like triathlons anyways.

The next mile seemed to take twice as long as the first four. At that point, another runner came chugging up beside me and said, "What's happening?"

"I'm dead," I replied. "I can't believe I didn't retire from this ten years ago."

He had the gall to say, "You're not doing so bad. Hang in there through this bad part and you'll get it going again."

I panted, "You go for it. I gotta stop."

"No," he said. "I'm staying with you for a while, then we'll see what happens." So he stayed with me, and somehow I kept going. I'm not sure whether it was his encouragement that kept me going or the guilt I knew I'd feel if I didn't stay with him, since he had slowed down to help me out.

He was right; it did get easier. The twenty pound weights myste-riously came off and I got going smoothly and effortlessly again. My friend ran on ahead of me after he saw that I was okay. About a mile later I was approaching a runner ahead of me who was struggling. When I caught up to him, I saw that it was my new friend. His face was pinched with fatigue, and his smooth stride had changed to a choppy, irregular beat. He was really struggling.

I said, "How's it going?"

71

He couldn't answer. His breaths were coming too fast to talk. He just waved me on. I didn't say anything. I just stayed with him until the finish line. We finished together, side-by-side, and afterwards hugged each other and exchanged names and addresses. Although we've never seen each other again, we'll be brothers for eternity.

Running had taken on a new meaning for me. No longer was it all for one and none for all. Work as hard as you can and kick everyone's butt. I got more satisfaction out of what had happened during that one race than I did out of all the races of my younger days combined. I had helped someone in need, and he had helped me when I was in need. The race was secondary to being human. Sometimes extraneous, competitive goals get in the way of what I really want to be: a loving, caring, sensitive person who would like to elevate those around him. No longer would I be so focused on what I wanted to do that I would miss out on what was going on around me.

After the race, I returned home to teach and coach, and I kept running, too. I began to see that the lesson I had learned should be applied to other areas of my life. I could see that there were times when other people in our school weren't running through their lives very smoothly. It seems we all have times when life attaches twenty pound weights that drag us down. That isn't the time when the rest of us, who are "running" well should turn the other way and run our own race. Teaching is a "people" profession, and we have to be careful to not get so focused on our own goals and programs that we lose sight of the big picture--the people picture. We have to reach out and encourage each other to keep trekking, to get through the tough times. After all, teaching is hard enough even when things are going well.

I suppose the toughest lesson I learned from running was that I had been so focused on achievement that I had missed out on the most rewarding part, the part about caring and being cared about.

I ran for a couple of months after that triathlon, until the inevitable injury occurred. I've missed the camaraderie of the running brotherhood. But Christmas is right around the corner again and my pants are getting a little tight.

11

Jargonasaurus II
(Intermediate Jargon)

As you recall, a couple of chapters previous I took on the challenge of giving teachers, new to the profession, an "enhanced" version of definitions for terms used by educators in the field. It was an attempt by me to fill a "void" in understanding between "book-learning" how to teach, and "real-world" practical use of the very same terms.

Because of the tremendous response (I had a letter from my grandmother admonishing me for being sarcastic), and also the test scores of the quiz I gave my readers, I feel like we are now prepared to move to the next, more sophisticated step: "Intermediate Jargon," (Jargonasaurus II).

The first chapter was intended, of course, to get the feet wet and inspire the learner to want to know more, which, judging by the overwhelming number of e-mails I have received, is why the following unabridged intermediate list is offered. After taking this seriously, teachers should, with study and practice, feel empowered (which is one of the terms now being used in a complete sentence) to carry on the highest level of conversations with all the pseudo-intellectuals at their school. (I meant regular people like me who try to teach, but I wanted to throw "pseudo" in there.)

Time Management--This is what everyone says we need to work on to be more efficient at our job. I have used the term many times

73

myself, in between cups of coffee and long-winded discourses on the decline of education in America.

Political Correctness--It means that you shouldn't say anything derogatory about someone, or a group of people, unless they are not used to it.

Empower(ment)--You will hear this word many times during workshops and conferences. It is sometimes used in relation to the teacher, but most often used with regard to getting "Johnny" to take more control of his own decision making. We do this by making rules and contracts for him to follow.

Constructive Criticism--This refers to suggestions a teacher is supposed to offer parents with regard to their offspring's classroom performance, maybe at a parent-teacher conference. There is a statistically significant difference between the types of suggestions offered by teachers who have children of their own and those who don't.

Educational Research--This is documented research that an educator looks up to prove that he was right all along. A good educator can find research to prove his point if he looks hard enough. Then he can use a phrase such as: "The research shows......" with much confidence because he knows that no one listening could possibly know if he was exaggerating or not. He should then follow up with something like: "This illustrates why everything we do here is 'data-driven.'"

"No Child Left Behind"--This is when students use instructional time to learn and practice test-taking skills rather than doing curricular work. This is helpful because it can improve a school's overall performance and also because we certainly wouldn't want curricular work to get in the way of their education.

Superintendent--(1) If you are employed in a large district, this is a person you probably haven't been introduced to yet. A written invitation to a meeting with this person has been known to cause digestive disorders. (2) The way to ameliorate your digestive disorders is to be prepared to show that you are "leaving no child behind."

Principal--This person is "in-charge" of what goes on in your school building. The harried look on his/her face is real. Most people don't realize that principals spend their vacations walking tightropes in the summer circus, which allows them to work on their most important job skill. If you look closely enough, you will see that they are attached by invisible strings to the superintendent you are unlikely to meet.

Short-term Memory--This characteristic is exhibited by some teachers who have become administrators.

Saving Money/Investments/Annuities--These are terms most teachers have no clue about. If you find out what they mean, would you call or write me, as I don't have a clue about them, either. Then we could include them in the advanced Jargonasaurus.

Consultant(s)--These are very smart people who are brought into your district to provide inservicing, or who may provide workshops where a group of teachers from your district will attend together with similar groups from other schools. Consultants are very smart because they are former teachers who are now making more money being consultants. You should pay attention to them.

"We're going to participate in a get-to-know-each-other activity"--This is how a consultant opens the workshop. The "activity" is really a set of activities designed to last until lunch, depending on how well-prepared the consultant is. If he/she is really prepared, these activities could last the whole day, making you happy that you attended, because now you know some previous strangers, a few of whom might have been working in the same building as you for the last three years.

Chain of Command--If you have a question/concern about something that happened in your room or building, you are expected to use this. A school's chain of command is similar to our present political system in that at each level (link of the chain), they listen to your question/concern, and then refer you up to the next link. The chain can be very long, but if you persevere and make it to the very end you will find no one there, only a memo stating: "The committee decided...." Since the committee has no face or telephone number, you can consider your problem solved and know that maybe you are the one that found the "missing link."

Micromanage--A school board member will tell you they won't do this, especially if you are not a personal friend.

Policy--This is what schools are expected to follow unless they have a reason not to. In that case, they will revise it.

Murphy's Law--This means that just about the time that you get used to your school district's grading program, it will be "upgraded."

Clause--No, this is not the pudgy guy in the red suit. It refers to a long forgotten phrase in your contract or insurance plan that comes back to bite you, as in: "Not covered by your copay," or "Other duties not previously assigned," and other similar statements.

Onus--interesting verbiage (not a body part) which, according to Webster, means "a burden placed on someone." Perhaps a sentence will help: The principal said, "The Onus is on us to get our test scores up," making me think of various body parts and functions in response.

"Thinking Outside the Box"--This is when we find another school district that has solved the problem we are currently dealing with, and we find out how they fixed it.

Mandate/Delegate--Words that end in –ate should make you nervous. These two words refer to requirements that descend from above, merge, and end up on your plate. The merging requires creativity and lots of paper shuffling and is why those people from above get paid more than we do.

Sexual Harassment/Discrimination--We are so lucky not to have to deal with this at our school. However, in the unlikely event that a teacher were involved in it, a district-wide memo would be sent out to everyone to solve the problem.

Raising the Bar--This means raising expectations of yourself and also of your students. Schools do this by signing up kids with low math scores in classes like Algebra II so they can catch up.

Acronyms--These are abbreviations like: ESE, ESOL, LEP, ACT, SAT, PDP, PLC, AYP, CYA, TLC, and many, many more. Ooops. I slipped a couple of extra ones in there. You will be extremely suave if you can remember what they all mean. If you can and you use them around old-timers like myself, and we start to stare off in the distance, maybe you could use a little TLC and remind us what they stand for.

Sauvivity--I saved this one for last because, well, I made it up myself. I am also working on a higher degree and need to practice this skill. This word relates to the confidence and smoothness with which you will use all the aforementioned terms when you converse with your compatriots.

Disclaimer--This is an indication that what is stated is not what's really meant. Disclaimers are used on insurance policies and teacher contracts, and sometimes in obituaries. This entire chapter should include the disclaimer that only the parts that made you smile, snicker, laugh, or just loudly guffaw are worth remembering because it was written with tongue firmly inserted in cheek. It's much easier for me to write with it that way.

So there you have it, and just in time, too. Just think, right after you read this intermediate version of the Jargonasaurus you might be having your "end-of- the-year" evaluation and you will be able to throw these terms around like a seasoned veteran.

Also, you are now prepared to deal with those teachers who may try to keep their "professional distance" (from you) by using snobby educational terms they think you won't understand. But you'll be able to derail such snobbishness with your own verbal swagger.

We will probably save terms like those for Jargonasaurus III, but if in the meantime you hear some really good ones, write me.

12

The Oat Bucket

Some of the best times of my early career were spent six miles from the nearest road. Walker Prairie is nestled in Wyoming's Bighorn Mountains. Every year in late August, my friend Lonnie and I backpacked in and left a camp set up until October. "Camp" consisted of a dome tent, a couple of sleeping bags, some canned foods, and some cookware. The camp was located next to Walker Creek, our water supply, which flowed along the west side of the prairie. When I finished teaching school on Fridays, we would pack some supplies and hike into camp. We hoped to find the majestic bugling bull elk, but mostly we enjoyed just being in the mountains.

Out there on Walker Prairie, I learned an important lesson from an old oat bucket. It occurred on the only trip in which we used pack horses. Were we excited! Without a sixty-pound pack to carry, we even had room for two 8x10 tents and wood stoves. No more cold feet or hopping around trying to get our pants on before freezing to death in the pre-dawn hours!

We loaded up the horses and started up Soldier Creek Trail. It didn't look so imposing without a pack on my back. The horses even let us hold their tails and dragged us up the steep parts. Upon arriving at camp, I still had enough energy to gather wood and start a campfire.

Denny, Lonnie's brother, and Willy, Denny's friend, had come along to help. (I found it interesting that we could never get them to help when we backpacked in.) After the horses were unpacked and camp was set up, we sat around congratulating ourselves that the horses made the trip so much easier for us. How nice it was to have a "real" camp with wood stoves and a cook tent!

As we celebrated, we decided to treat the horses to thank them for such an enjoyable experience. So Willy went to feed the horses some oats.

The next thing we heard was the thundering of running hooves. We scrambled to the door of the cook tent in time to glimpse the south end of three horses disappearing toward the north end of Walker Prairie. *Hmmm, this might be a good time for me to disappear*, I thought, as steam began to emerge from Lonnie's ears. We were soon hiking north on a quest for three horses. With Denny and Willy searching fringe timber and Lonnie and me in the middle of the prairie, we scavenged its length and found no sign of them.

I sure was glad we had brought the horses along in order to save energy for our overall effort, but my comment to that effect didn't exactly cheer up my partners. We were about to give up the quest when I spied the top of a ridge with a plush meadow. "I'll bet they're up there," I said. I climbed the hill, found the horses knee-deep in plush mountain grass, and motioned to the others. We formed a semicircle and got almost close enough to touch the critters. Evidently they decided to play tag, because just as we reached to put ropes around their necks, they took off in the direction of camp. We followed their tracks back but lost them. Exhausted, we returned to camp and pondered our next move.

Since the horses belonged to Lonnie and Denny, the next step was theirs. "Leave 'em," Lonnie said. "They're more trouble than they're worth. 'Sides, Willy lost 'em. Let him find 'em," he continued. Sensing Lonnie's growing anger, I gently suggested to Willy that this might be a good time to find something to do outside the tent. As he left, he picked up the oat bucket and grabbed a stick. I wondered if his guilt caused him to think he didn't deserve to eat human food. Before I could say anything, though, Willy started banging on the bucket with the stick.

Then the most amazing thing happened. Three horses came running to Willy in less than twenty seconds. Looking like nothing had ever happened, they followed him into the corral and docilely began munching their oats. Every few seconds they would turn to look at us as if to say, *Why's everybody staring? Haven't you ever seen a horse eat oats before?*

I've never forgotten that oat bucket lesson. When problems arise, I remind myself that they're rarely as big as they seem. Before rushing off to solve them, it can help to detach yourself from the situation and try to find a simple solution. The oat bucket taught me how to deal with life, including my teaching life, realistically.

For example, when Travis Petty joined my earth science class, I spent the first few days observing him to discover what kind of kid he was. I also checked his records to explore his past. "This one's a real loser," I heard someone say. "He's seventeen and still in the ninth grade. Why are we getting more of these types lately?"

Travis really bugged me. Polite and fairly articulate with me and the other teachers, he did everything in class except work. He demanded constant attention from his peers. This need interfered with his ability to learn science, while also distracting the other students and me. I had encountered disruptive students before and had usually handled them effectively, but Travis was different. I tried the one-on-one chat after class, isolation, and phone calls. He would agree that his behavior needed to change.

The next day I'd start class expecting a change, and Travis would come up and say, "Mr. B, I forgot my pencil and book. You got any extra paper?" And so it went. As I struggled to find a way to reach Travis, I was banging on the bucket in the same old way, but he was only looking--not running toward it.

When parent conferences arrived, Mrs. Petty came in without a Mr. Petty. As I explained grading policies and behavior expectations, Mrs. Petty began to sob. "Travis's dad isn't home," she explained. "He just up and left a couple of years ago, and we haven't seen him since. Travis hasn't been the same. I can't get him to do anything he should, and he hasn't passed but a couple of classes since it happened."

I wanted to cry, too, as I considered Travis's situation. Then I looked at the rest of my students, trying to understand whether family situations might interfere with their school work. I discovered that over 50 percent of our student body came from single-parent families. Another 20 percent, although both parents were still together, suffered from dysfunctional settings.

That meant that 70 percent of my students had severe family problems. Some were able to overcome these situations and do well academically. But a high percentage were not performing near their potential, and many were failing classes. I wondered what "normal" means when referring to kids today. What does "teaching the average kid" mean when there is no "average"?

I wanted to hold out "the bucket" to these students, but I didn't know how to bang on it or what to put in it. I wondered how to teach science past staring, far-away eyes and to kids who were just plain hard and angry. I felt helpless and inadequate.

Several problems face teachers in trying to relate to kids from single-parent homes. Most of us grew up when children usually had both parents in the home. In addition, most veteran educators began their careers teaching students from traditional families.

A second problem is that undergraduate teacher training is woefully behind in dealing with ever-increasing numbers of single parents and educational obstacles caused by a lack of family structure. It's time to replace timeworn material with insights on handling kids with these special problems. Consider this a cry for help to the powers that be:

Please help experienced and new teachers develop innovative ways to bang on the bucket.

With more kids living with only their mothers, the third problem is an even greater need for male teachers who will commit themselves to being role models. We need many more male teachers in elementary and middle schools willing to help "father" children who never had a dad or who have lost the one they had. A student to teacher friendship may be the only solid relationship a child has with an adult.

Our school formed an "at risk" committee to identify these children and to develop individualized strategies to help them. Some teachers volunteered to "watch out" for three or four of them on a daily basis. This plan built solid adult-child relationships and developed some structure so often missing in a child's life.

For example, when Traci fell apart at basketball practice, I had no idea why. After practice she stayed to talk with me, asking, "Coach, is something wrong with me?" She was our best player, but was extremely moody. I asked her what she meant. Traci had a tendency to build friendships and soon find a way to mess them up. "No one likes me," she said.

"How're things going at home?" I asked. I knew there had been some long-term problems.

"My dad and mom aren't going to get back together like I hoped. I don't know what I did to make them so mad."

It seemed silly to me that this senior thought she was the reason her parents were splitting up. Traci was the eleventh child, and the parents had stayed together until only she was left at home. I wanted to put on a football referee shirt, go over to their house to throw the red flag on their carpet and yell, "Interference!"

"Traci, listen to me," I said. "Your parents split up because they have their own problems. You aren't the problem. You're letting their problems creep into the way you treat your friends. Because you're not sure of your parents' love, you doubt that anyone could love you, so maybe you're doing weird things to find out if they care or not. Traci, you're okay. Got it?"

I couldn't think of anything else to say or do except give this weeping girl a hug and hope she understood what I had told her.

Although some wounds she carries may be permanent, Traci did make progress during the year.

We teachers need to get to know our students who have special needs and meet them if we can. It's not enough to punch in and out, doing good "teacher things" like setting high expectations, using "data-driven" techniques, reaching closure, and doing cooperative learning.

Perhaps we could have taught most kids the same way in the past, but times have changed and so have kids and families. Therefore, we need to change, to put the right stuff in the bucket and bang on it so every kid will come running. When we learn to do that, we need to share what we've learned with our colleagues because we're all in the same "camp," even if it isn't in such a "next to heaven" place like Walker Prairie, Wyoming.

Let's have an extra ounce of compassion for these kids, translating it into time spent with them. Let's not avoid talking with them about their problems when they want to talk. Let's tell them that sometimes life isn't fair, but the opportunity is there for them to make something of it if they really want to.

13

Rhondaisms

Rhonda took two classes from me one year, chemistry and human biology. These were two of the hardest classes in the school. She was one of those hard cases that you can see coming your way from the junior high, and you wonder if you should take early retirement before she gets to your level. She was a big girl, around 5 feet 9 inches tall, large around but not obese, very stout, loud, and intimidating to her classmates and most of the adults. She had spent her share of time in in-school detention and out-of-school suspensions for physical and emotional confrontations of every sort imaginable.

Well, I couldn't afford to retire at thirty-eight years of age, and I couldn't find another job, had a low number of sick days (sometimes called "mental health days" by creative teachers), so here I was sucking it up and teaching Rhonda chemistry and human biology.

I knew a little bit about Rhonda's past: trouble with her parents, previously being sent to a private religious school against her will, ever-increasing tendency toward violent behavior, abusive to teachers and other authority figures, and daily run-ins with just about everyone. Needless to say, there was plenty to worry about when Rhonda came through the door, and she rarely missed school.

Using my best "teacher psychology techniques," I thought I should try to persuade Rhonda that it should be her idea that chemistry and human biology might be too strenuous of a workload for her. Of course I was sensitive to the fact that she might put me in a "full nelson" headlock to get her own way, so as an alternative, when she objected, I let her talk me out of it.

After having Rhonda in class for a quarter, I had learned that there were really two Rhondas. There was the one with the tough exterior, which I've already described. One of the toughest parts of her exterior was her colorful and creative use of the English language. She used her understanding of the language to make sure all authority figures understood who was actually in control of her life. A few of those especially in-your-face remarks made me laugh, so I call them "Rhondaisms." Some of my favorites were:

> "This school sucks," which was a regular.
> "I hate school."
> "Are we going to learn anything from this?"
> "You scum."
> "Why do we have stupid homework?"

These were just a few of the tasteful examples of things she might express in my class. I was known to occasionally have something to say back like, "Morning, Rhonda. Why don't you tell us how you really feel?" or "If you're going to give your opinion on something, I wish you would quit beating around the bush and get it out in the open."

This usually lightened the mood; we had a laugh and got on with class. I realized that the other kids probably thought the same things as Rhonda expressed, but kept it to themselves. In a way, I felt better that more than one kid would think I was scum. In spite of it all, I appreciated Rhonda for her directness and honesty.

What you saw was what you got. In a "committee, site-based oriented" approach to making decisions in schools, it was refreshing to hear someone that told the truth as she saw it. I hoped that the direct approach was a particular character trait others would see in me. But ... back to the other Rhonda.

The "other" Rhonda really surprised me. This was the conscientious Rhonda. No student asked for more help, came in more often to retake quizzes and tests, bugged me to make sure she had all of her assignments turned in, and kept track of her progress as much as Rhonda. Go figure.

That was the part of Rhonda I was not expecting. I had encountered hard cases before, but they always were unconcerned and unmotivated academically. Rhonda had potential like all kids, but unlike most, she knew it and had a pretty good idea of what it was. She hated school more than most, but didn't let the hatred stop her from becoming something. She might have been aware that only school could provide her a way out of what made her the way she was, the environment she lived in, but that's only a personal hypothesis. She was a refreshing break from any mold or category of kid I'd ever known.

There was no pretense, no brown-nosing, no facades. She learned the information, got the grades, and hated my guts. I liked it, I really did. Most of the time we have to play this game with kids, with these rules: Let them know we like them, hoping they like us back so they will listen and cooperate more than they would if they didn't like us and, as a result, they will be successful at school.

Too many teachers get frustrated with kids who aren't "attached" to them and respond academically, when it is their own fault for setting up the rules of the game in the first place. It bored me to play that game, and Rhonda allowed me to be just a teacher, and in its own weird sort of way that was a rare treat.

The one thing that bothered me about Rhonda was that she hated school. I tried really hard not to let that penetrate my thickening skin, but it still bothered me. I remembered saying, back in the old days, that I hated school, too, but I really didn't. I would have been bored to death if it weren't for school. School provided a break in the sometimes monotonous routine of irritating my parents and siblings at home, and allowed me to irritate my teachers at school instead.

In addition, I enjoyed the activities and company of my friends who also provided a certain entertainment level for me when they got in trouble at school. Once in a while we even learned something and enjoyed it, but it would have been hard to admit.

I wondered what made kids hate school or say they did. I would spend a little time over at the elementary school once in awhile, and it was clear that the littlest kids loved school. But by the time they got to high school, the percentage of kids who would say they hated school was pretty high.

What happens to kids between the third grade and the ninth grade to make them this way? Does the "Dark Side of the Force" invoke some sort of hate mechanism, or is there some set of circumstances that occurs to kids who hate school, as opposed to those who still like it? Is it hormonal? Is it because of fear of failure? Is it me?

I was provided with some insight into this situation when my own son, Nathan, came home from school and announced that he "hated school." At about the same time, my wife and I were invited to one of those parent-teacher conferences they have a couple times a year. A little anxious about why we were invited, we grilled Nate on what had been going on at school. He was upset about a "timed test" he had taken in arithmetic. He was in the fourth grade at the time, and a very good math student. He had nearly completed thirty questions in a "mad minute." I was impressed. I doubted I could have done that well.

The problem, in Nate's mind, was that he had missed the second question on the "mad minute" test, as a result of which the teacher had only given him credit for one question correct, despite the fact that he had the other twenty-eight questions after that correct.

I could appreciate the teacher's reasoning. She was trying to convey that it's more important to get the answers correct than it is to race through a task and make lots of mistakes. I could see the wisdom of it because I'm an adult and a teacher.

Nate couldn't, and although I liked school just fine, Nate had just turned a certain corner and decided he didn't really like school anymore. In Nate's fourth grade mind, math was his thing, his niche in his class, something he was really smart at, and that test scoring method had hurt him and his pride in his "standing." After we tried to explain the reasoning of the teacher to him, he asked us in tears, "Shouldn't we get credit for what we do right instead of be punished for the ones we get wrong?"

I had no answer. I knew he was right. He's a very bright kid, and this episode made me a better teacher as a result of his pain. In our infinite wisdom as educators, we have to be aware of the effect on our students of the seemingly insignificant things we do, even the way we correct and score papers.

Nate gave me more insight into teaching one day when he came home, now in middle school. "How did school go today?" was the usual obligatory question.

"Okay, I guess."

I asked him what the problem was. He said, "Mrs. Finch likes to teach, but she doesn't like kids."

Whammo! It hit me right between the eyes. Some of those kids who got to high school, already hating school, had a teacher along the way that didn't like kids.

We teachers might be the problem. I might be the problem.

We might find it refreshing to not have to play the "liking game," but it's not refreshing at all for kids. I'm talking about "loving" kids in general, as a group, defining that love as: Doing what's in their best interest no matter what.

Oh, we may teach the curriculum very well. We can attend in-services and workshops, correct papers, and do lesson plans all night long. We can use all the newest language and reading techniques and buy into whatever our school district tells us to. We can score very well on formative and summative evaluations and every year get a contract. But we can still flunk the "Love Test," and kids can read that better than any book.

Like it or not, young children need an emotional connection to the adult teaching them, and if they don't get that, they may perceive it as some sort of rejection, and begin to associate the negative emotion with school. From that point on, students who experience these feelings may become more difficult to teach and more difficult to reconnect with.

One day a friend of mine asked one of my teacher-colleagues, "What do you teach?" probably expecting him to say something like: "Chemistry."

"I teach kids," he said.

I remember that answer like it was yesterday. Always will.

We teach the whole person, and to a great degree, we are responsible for the development of that person. Most of the great teachers I know teach because they love kids, and are determined to make a positive difference in their lives.

I loved Rhonda. I particularly loved her up-front style. But I hoped that I would never cause a single kid to feel the way she did about school.

Postscript: I first drafted this chapter in 1990. In 1999, I saw Rhonda when I had an appointment at the hospital. She was an RN. Her supervisor said she was an excellent nurse. Victory is sweet. I savored Rhonda's victory for a long time after that. I still do.

···· 14 ····

The Line

It was June, 2001. I was standing in line, a very long line, at an event called "The Great Florida TeachIn," which was a teacher recruitment fair where representatives of almost all the school districts in Florida would gather on a weekend and allow "wanna-be" teachers to meet them and do on-site interviews. In many cases, jobs were offered on the spot.

I was one of the older wanna-bees, with twenty-three years of experience under my belt, but I felt apprehension, similar to the naïve youngsters I saw streaming from place to place in groups moving sort of like amoebas to and from different district booths, especially those with the higher starting pay. I watched and waited, with around 3,000 other people.

Standing in line appeals to me, rating right up there with going to the dentist to get a root canal, or with the nerve conduction test I just had on my ulnar nerve where the technician said, with a sardonic smile, "You're gonna feel this one, so get ready."

As I was waiting in line, I drifted off into "who knows where," and it dawned on me that we spend a lot of time in lines. I think I read somewhere how many hours a day we do certain activities like eating, sleeping, watching TV, etc. I remember a former professor trying to impress on us college students how much time is left to do some studying, even after we do all the things we shouldn't be doing. I also read somewhere that an astronomical amount of fuel is wasted while people sit in their cars, in lines, at traffic lights. I wonder if anyone ever did any research on how much time people stand in lines.

Don't get me wrong. Not all standing in lines is completely awful. One of the more enjoyable and most distant memories I have is when we had to stand in line in elementary school, sometimes holding hands with a member of the other gender. I found this to be okay, particularly when it was Mary Mahoney, my third grade sweetheart, although she never was aware of it.

Still drifting, I recalled several "personal" days I took while teaching in a Wyoming ranch town, having offered to help with a sheep-shearing event. In the heart of Basque country, it was not out of the ordinary for a large ranch to have several thousand sheep to shear in the spring.

When they did, they usually imported a private shearing operation, which consisted of seven or eight New Zealanders who stood with their electric tools in a semi-truck trailer that had been set up to force sheep into a line and up a ramp and over to one of the eight shearers to get sheared in about two minutes and then onto a down-ramp to join their much skinnier buddies. My job was to use an electronic prod to keep the flock moving in single file up the ramp to the shearers. It was amazing that we could shear over 800 sheep in one day.

"Mister, could you move ahead and keep up?" the young man behind me in line said as he brought me back to the present. I wanted to say, "Baaaaa."

Drifting again, I was back in college, standing in line, trying to get registered for classes--of course waiting until the last minute to get it done. Seeing several stations lined up in sort of a sequence, I figured this to be an "entrance intelligence/problem solving" test to see who was the smartest, so I skipped a couple of unnecessary stations and advanced to the fourth station where it said something like "financial aid."

"You need your class schedule, Mr. Biebel. You'll have to go back to station one." Hmmm, well, part of the learning process is realizing when you can and can't take shortcuts. *This must be part of my "real" education*, I thought. Getting registered in college, at least the way we did it, had to be about as rewarding as the process of getting sheared was to a sheep.

"Dan, are you going to move with the rest of the amoebas or what?" My wife, Cheri, who was at the Great Florida TeachIn with me, brought me out of that past nightmare into the present. "Baaaa…" I said.

"What?" She had already had two interviews, and I was still hanging out in line.

"Almost there, almost there," I repeated, kinda like Luke Skywalker about to blow up the Death Star.

"Hello, Mr. Bible. It's very good to meet you today," the shearer said. I had arrived at the desk of a very friendly principal, Mrs. Windermere, from Galberry High School. It was okay that she mispronounced my name. Don't all the sheep look and sound alike by now?

We went to a desk in sort of a cubicle where she sat on one side of a table looking at my paperwork, asking appropriate questions about my experience, style of teaching, how to handle discipline, and other things I expected. There were at least twelve of these cubicles where different representatives, in close proximity, were all asking pretty much the same questions of different people at the same time, somehow trying to fit their needs with the highest quality applicant they could find, sorting out one from the other according to some criteria known only to them.

Some of the districts used a "canned" approach, where they asked everyone the same questions and rated them on some numerical scale. Lots of prospective teachers there that day seemed to have been groomed in advance to know what the questions and the answers were supposed to be.

"Baaaa…" I whined. Unfortunately, this left me at a disadvantage, since I hadn't attended a "wannabe teacher" class for a long time, so I wasn't very well groomed in advance.

One of the questions I did know that we were supposed to have prepared an answer to beforehand was: What is your philosophy of education? So I asked myself: *If I am an administrator trying to interview umpteen prospective teachers in a day to try and sort them out, would I have time to even pretend to read some eloquent discourse on my role in the upbringing of America's youth?*

Realizing this, my simple response was: "Kids come first, and kids need as many options as possible to be successful in coping and adapting to a fast-changing world." That was it. I had three job offers by the end of the day.

The next several days, though, having not accepted any of the jobs, I had time to ponder the issue of just what my philosophy of education really was. Beyond that, what did my philosophy of education have to do with good teaching, and how would it translate into good teaching?

As a result of visiting with well-respected teachers that I have known and having observed their strategies and techniques, I realize that a philosophy of education and good teaching techniques are interwoven, and the following factors are foundational:

Kids must come first. A practical philosophy of education pictures students exiting their formal education with skills that allow them as many options as possible to be successful in coping and adapting to a constantly changing world. Good teachers do their jobs in such a way as to enhance this process. They are able to see the "big picture" of the needs of a whole person while at the same time developing a knowledge base in different content areas.

Good teachers do the following:

Communicate well and on the level of the listener. They have high and appropriate expectations of all learners, and these can vary from student to student. They can and will provide interesting activities in different styles. They ask questions on different levels depending on the ability of the listeners. They promote and model the concept of being life-long learners. They assess and monitor student progress and adjust or adapt to the speed with which the learner can assimilate knowledge and concepts.

Good teachers are prepared every day with a lesson that will take the whole class period. They are able to control their classes and use appropriate methods, prepared in advance, to prevent critical incidents from happening. They have energy and enthusiasm, and rarely sit during a class.

Good teachers use technology in the classroom, are positive with kids, honest with everyone, and are smart enough to know when to share information and when not to.

Good teachers can accept the fact that there will be times when administrators will require paperwork and participation in activities or duties that seem "worthless." While it may seem that these activities and duties have nothing to do with teaching or learning, good teachers are able to contribute and finish these tasks on time, adhering to school policies, while expecting students to do so also.

Good teachers are able to maintain confidentiality.

Good teachers like kids. They enjoy being with them, and as a result they have good rapport with them.

Good teachers have a sense of humor. They don't take themselves too seriously, are flexible to a point, and they can work in teams as followers or as leaders.

Good teachers can take "no" for an answer.

Good teachers enjoy teaching.

These are my observations, having passed through the long line of the pre-school student, through primary, secondary, college, and post-graduate formal education, and now as a facilitator. I hope that this practical student-centered philosophy that I have gleaned from other great teachers will help me direct the part of the line that comes to me and keep those who are in the line moving in the right direction.

And, if you ever have the assignment of using the "prod" to keep the sheep moving forward, don't worry ... they feel a lot better when that thick layer of fleece comes off.

········ *15* ········

Bridges

"Hey Beeb, you ready yet?" It was the voice of Sam French, who was calling me to find out if I was ready to lead the Windsor High School "Yellowjacket" cross country team in its first practice of the season.

It was a warm, sunny, September afternoon in this sleepy Vermont town, which sits at the base of Mount Ascutney, hemming it up against the Connecticut River. This 100-yard-wide, deep, fast-moving river separates Vermont from New Hampshire along their entire mutual border. As the captain of the team, it was my job to keep everyone together as we jogged and then ran on our first run of the season, seeing to it that no one slacked and also that no one left everyone "in the dust," for this was a traditional run at Windsor High School, the first one marking the beginning of a new season, one to be taken with seriousness and a sort of reverence. This run was meant to be taken together.

Our first practice of every season was to run down to the river and cross the famous Windsor-Cornish Covered Bridge, renowned as the longest two-span covered bridge in the world. At our age, we didn't reflect much on the special standing of the bridge as, by the time we got there, there were a bunch of out of shape guys who had not much conscious thought of any kind, much less energy to reflect on the historical status of this bridge.

The sign over the entrance says: "Walk your horses or pay a two dollar fine."

We only wished we had horses at that point, and as we ran across the bridge we could look down through the holes between the floor planks and see the river moving to the right underneath us. It could cause vertigo if you looked too long.

In the middle of the bridge there was a rock pillar supporting the center of the bridge, where the two spans connected. Here there was a ladder, leading from a trap door in the wall down to the base, just barely above the water. "Hey, bet you guys don't dare to climb down there with me," said Fred Lester.

"Let's keep going," I said. "We still got the hardest part in front of us." I think this conversation was part of the tradition as well.

The hardest part was about a half mile north on Route 12A, on the New Hampshire side where there is a dirt road called "Slade Road" that takes an angle off the main road to the right and heads at about a fifty degree slope up Dingleton Hill.

Our job, the traditional first workout, was to run up this hill about 200 yards, jog back to the bottom, repeating three times. We did the job, knees to chest, leaning forward into the hill, pumping arms, not looking up, starting fast and light and finishing slow and heavy, barely able to lift our legs near the top, breathing loud and long, chests heaving and standing around bent over with hands on our knees, trying to collect our collective breath while waiting for everyone to make it, either running or walking.

When everyone was finished, we would slap each other high fives and on the back, walk to the bottom of the hill, and then jog back across the bridge and on back to school. We had successfully started a new season and school year at Windsor High School and everyone was still alive to say so.

There are some other bridges that have a significant place in my life's tapestry. I can still remember Grandpa Biebel telling all of us that the George Washington Bridge in New York City was the third longest extension bridge in the United States when we first went across it on a visit to the city when I was very young and we were heading to the World's Fair in New York City. I didn't know if Grandpa had his facts right or not, but for this Vermont country boy, it was a very impressive event, crossing a bridge that seemed like it took forever to get to the other side of and under which you could see huge ships passing by at the same time.

Another very impressive bridge structure that amazes me and reminds me of the limitless possibilities of humankind and what can be done if something really has to get done is the Sunshine Skyway Bridge south of St. Petersburg, Florida. It lifts up to the sky over the water in a beautiful, angelic, and heavenly arch that says without words, "You can do whatever you set your mind to do" and "I will get you to the other side" at the same time.

I can think of a couple of less significant bridges that I have used that don't serve the general public. One is a simple, twisting log about eight inches in diameter that just happened to be in the right place at the right time for my friend Ed and I to get across a Wyoming creek from one side to the other.

"There's a spot. We can get across there," Ed said, and he bounded across it without another thought. For me it wasn't so simple. Being afraid of heights and not the most coordinated klutz in the world, it took a lot of coaxing from Ed, but I finally made it across, arms stretched out to both sides, jerking around to keep my balance like a high-wire performer, even though I was only two feet above the water.

For him, the log bridge was a way across the river; for me it was that and also a way of overcoming fear. You see, bridges can serve more than one purpose.

Sometimes bridges, especially natural ones, can serve the purpose of humbling the individual trying to traverse them. Not long after my confidence-building log crossing with Ed, I took my sons Branden and Nate trout fishing with my teacher and friend, Randy Thompson and his son Randy Jr., on the Red Fork of the Powder River, a blue-ribbon trout stream if there ever was one. After fishing for awhile, we came to a small but deep pool where the water was blocked by a large cottonwood log to force water down an irrigation ditch, when the rancher chose to open the headgate, allowing water to run into his irrigation system.

The gate was closed that day, and the water was passing between the log and the rocks supporting it, with a little stream about two feet wide crossing over the log, falling into a rocky pool about four feet below.

What we had was the end of our fishing trip, because the water was too deep above the log and too fast just below it to cross. Not to be denied, and with a new found confidence in log walking, I proudly declared that I would cross the log, even with my waders on. I made it to the wet center, whereupon both my feet went out from under me, and with not too much class, I fell the four feet onto the rocks below and into the deep pool, and to add creative tension to the situation, I allowed my chest waders to fill up with water while my head was under.

Leaving discretion to the wind, Randy jumped in and helped me out of the water. Of course I was fighting him off, swearing that I had seen a huge rainbow trout and was trying to get a better look--a human fishfinder, if you will. I broke two ribs on that one, so for quite some time, coughing and sneezing were my reminders not to be so foolish in the future.

Sometimes bridges appear in the strangest places. In the Big Horn National Forest above Sheridan, Wyoming, there is a trail, a rough trail, that leads from a passable road to the south end of Walker Prairie, a long, beautiful meadow seven miles from the nearest road, which is home to some great fishing, hiking, camping, and hunting opportunities.

To get to the prairie, one has to hike, ride a four wheeler, or take a horse down the famous Game Creek Trail, which has a hill on it called "Muffler Hill." That name should tell you why you don't take your regular vehicle, and also why it's famous.

The road ends at the south end of Walker Prairie, where a beautiful mountain stream called Big Goose Creek flows from the snow-capped peaks of the Big Horns down to the Sheridan area below. Right there, at the end of Game Creek Trail, is a bridge in the middle of nowhere, a beautiful bridge, with a cement walkway, steps, and steel supports and handrails, allowing people on foot or horseback to pass over the creek without getting soaked in the frigid, fast-moving mountain water.

Every time I crossed that bridge, I was extremely thankful for its presence and marveled at the effort, expense, and time it must have taken to build that bridge so far from the nearest road.

I love "draw bridges" as well. There is a big draw bridge on the Housatonic river between Stratford and Milford, Connecticut, the two towns my grandparents lived in. It was a hopeful time for me when I was little, traveling between my two sets of grandparents' homes, hoping the drawbridge would be up so I could see a big ship or sailboat passing by. That bridge had a distinct humming sound when you went over its metal grid. I liked that and tried to hum along.

There is a drawbridge in the town I live in now as well, and it serves a different, higher purpose for me. Let me try to explain. On the way to school every morning I have to drive across Taylor Creek, which has a small drawbridge over it, just long enough for a sailboat to cross under the bridge on its way out to Lake Okeechobee, Florida. Every workday as I pass over this bridge at approximately 6:30 AM, it serves as a reminder to start a morning prayer.

The prayer is an attempt, a very human attempt, of a teacher who is about to enter a school world that will have a new, unique day full of opportunities, challenges, conflicts, successes, and failures. I am not always emotionally prepared to enter that world; in fact, most days not. Hence the bridge; hence the prayer.

The prayer goes something like this: "Thank you Lord for the day, as I know that You have made it, and since You did make it, You certainly have the power to help me make it through the day. Thank You for this job and the opportunity I have to have a positive impact on the lives of young people. Help me, Lord, so that what I do and say would bring honor, and not dishonor, to Your Name. Help me to have the characteristics that good teachers have, such as patience, understanding, and a sense of humor. Help me to be productive, and not lazy. Please help me fight negativity and the tendency to be critical of others; rather, help me be part of the solution and not the problem. Help me to have compassion, and yet still be firm. Help me to have integrity in my interactions. Please help me find a positive way to handle certain students (naming names), and help them understand and respond to what I am trying to do with them. Help me to have their best interests at heart and not my own."

The prayer goes on to include members of my family, people who are sick, and other current issues that I am concerned about.

Bridges are really cool. They can serve us in so many ways. This bridge is a reminder to me every day, to start the day by laying out all my cares before God, and it releases me from some of the stresses that interfere with my productive abilities and the internal conflicts I feel that can contribute to depression and a lack of effectiveness as a person and teacher.

The prayer is my "Bridge over Troubled Waters," and I am thankful that that little drawbridge is there to remind me to use it.

16

Backpacks

Principal Weston, Mrs. Bernstein, Superintendent Justice, members of the school board, parents, and, of course, members of the graduating class. I was not offended that you didn't ask me to give the commencement address this year, but I made one up anyway. I thought I would take this opportunity to share it with you (including my notes to myself).

I am honored that I have your attention now, and I promise that this will not take as long as a root canal to accomplish, as I pass on what little I know of value.

If I could pick out one thing that has changed the most in the last few decades since I began teaching, I would have a lot to choose from. There's the music. We used to be able to understand the lyrics to the meaningless songs we listened to, but now, finally, we have removed that obstacle and allowed the music itself to minister directly to our soul, so that's an improvement.

The manner in which the music has changed its delivery is amazing, is it not? Back "in our day," we used to huddle around a phonograph with a turntable that played 45s (singles), 33 1/3s (albums), and 78s as it scratched its way through the songs, which were sometimes hard to understand, even though it was very exciting to be on the technological edge. If you have no idea what I am talking about, please ask someone my age--if you can find them. Now we have phonographs the size of a matchbox that a student can hide in his pocket and, if sneaky enough, maybe by wearing a hooded sweatshirt, can listen to with earphones all day while pretending to pay attention to class presentations and such.

The clothes have changed quite a bit as well. They have gone from bellbottoms with flowers or plaids in the 60s to today's pants/shorts that, well, hang below the buttocks, while wearing the hooded sweat shirt with a set of wires which comes up, eventually leading to the ears. I'm not sure which was better. Yes, students' looks have changed a lot in forty years or so, but that isn't the biggest change.

Consider the difference in modes of transportation, then and now. In the 60s and 70s students with licenses drove to school in GTOs, Mustangs, or they rode in on tiny little motor scooters called "Vespas." Although kids still like the sporty types of vehicles, we now have pickup trucks, and not the ones that you buy to do work around the farm. These trucks have big tires, and they're jacked up in the back, stereo pounding loud enough to cause the Richter Scale to blush. This is the vehicle used to cruise Main Street looking for some action at nighttime.

But this isn't the biggest change, either.

The biggest change I have noticed during my teaching career is (drumroll) the backpack. [Hoist backpack up from under the podium and put it on the table.] Every student in every class period comes to my class with a backpack. This is their method of keeping track of pretty much all of their stuff. Of course, it might be scary to look and see what's in there, but one might expect to find some books (possibly)--in very good shape I might add; almost looking like they haven't been out of the pack since the first day of school. Then there are occasional notebooks [continue the illustration] with not many pages containing writing, some pencils never sharpened, a calculator (hey, this looks like it belongs to a teacher), a cell phone still on, an assortment of dried-up foods, melted candies, and, if you look way down there at the bottom, perhaps something that is moving!

The benefit of the backpack is obvious. It keeps students from having to carry all this stuff around in their arms like we used to, and it eliminates the possibility of the humiliation of spilling everything onto the ground right in front of that cute girl, Gretchen, we were hoping to impress. Not cool. [Hold the backpack up.] Holding the backpack up with both hands, I judge the average weight to be, oh, not more than forty or fifty pounds. No wonder our chiropractor is doing so well in this town.

But I digress. The first "carrying thing" I ever had was a Bug's Bunny Lunchbox. [Hold up Bugs Bunny Lunchbox.] I had one in the second grade when I attended Maple Avenue Elementary in Claremont, New Hampshire. I lived about a half mile from the school, and the first day I had the lunchbox I was proud as could be and raced to school to show off my lunchbox.

The next day held even more promise because my Mom had bought me my very own Roadrunner thermos. This would certainly raise my stature in my class, as I would be the only one with warm soup to have with my peanut butter and jelly sandwich from my Bugs Bunny lunchbox. As fate would have it, as I raced toward school, stepping in all the mudpuddles, of course, I tripped, fell, and broke my thermos--they were made of glass in those days--on the edge of the sidewalk. I was heartbroken and cried all the way back home. My Mom, understanding that I was emotionally distraught, and for good reason, let me stay home for the day.

The next "carrying thing" I remember was when I went on a hike out in the woods behind Paradise Park with Preston Sweeney. Preston was a couple of years older than me, and he was willing to show me the way of the woodsman. He introduced me to whittling, the proper method of hacking down trees with a hatchet, how to start a fire without a match (which for some reason we never accomplished), and all the various uses of a Swiss Army knife.

The things that Preston taught me are too numerous for this speech, but the best thing he had going for him was that he had an "Army" backpack. [Hold up an old Army backpack.] Yes, he was clear on that, he had picked it up at the War Surplus store. It was green, heavy canvas with two straps over the cover that he

105

pulled though a metal clasp, then pulled tight so everything was secure. The best part was that you could wear it on your back, keeping your hands free to do all kinds of kid things, like digging a cave, or scrambling up a tree, etc. This was way more practical than my Bugs Bunny Lunchbox.

Fast forward a few years and you will find me in Wyoming, being introduced to the outdoor way by Denny Brestin, the first student outdoorsman I met in my teaching career. He took it upon himself to teach me how to be a successful outdoorsman. While I will not divulge all the particulars, which will safeguard my reputation, such as it is, I will admit that he taught me that I needed:

- a garage full of the best outdoor gear, which included several backpacks;
- a light daypack [hold up day pack], which was handy for carrying only the necessities needed for one day;
- a fanny pack [hold up fanny pack], useful for short trips;
- bigger backpack [hold up bigger pack], with waist belt for heavier things that might include a water supply;
- a pack frame, with an adjustable shelf [hold up], with a waist belt for carrying really heavy loads.

In the earlier days, when I was in shape, and the shape wasn't round, I was not intimidated about carrying heavy loads on long treks, provided they were packed right. Within a short time, I reviewed my strategy and discovered I liked hiking in the woods a lot better with as little weight as possible, so I spent a lot of my problem-solving energy on figuring out what I could do without.

This was not true of all my hiking friends, Tom Nordstrom being a fine example. Tom had come up from the city to hike with me. We got out of the truck together at 6:00 AM. There was a slight chill in the air (about 20 degrees) and a whisper of snow on the ground (maybe a foot and a half). We were being left off at a trailhead on Rockchuck Pass and were going to hike halfway to the bottom of the mountain, spend the night in a tent and sleeping bags, and then go the rest of the way the next day to a car that would be left waiting for us at the other end of the trail. It was an excellent plan.

We donned our packs and headed down the trail, thankful that we would be going downhill most of the day. After an hour or so, we did have to climb a small rise (a half mile hill at about a 40 degree angle). I looked behind, and Tom was lagging--slowly trudging up the hill, all stooped over.

"How's it going?" I inquired.

"Man, this pack is heavy, and my feet are killing me," he replied.

I helped him take his pack off.

"Whatcha got in here, a rock collection?" I asked.

"Just a bunch of stuff, just in case."

Well, Tom had everything in the pack: canned food (enough for three days), three different first aid kits, a heavy frying pan, and a couple of utensil kits. Under the pack was his sleeping bag, the tent, and one of those cool roll up mats you can sleep on. All told, the pack weighed at least sixty pounds. No wonder he was tired.

Sensing impending doom, meaning we would never make it if he was to continue like this, it occurred to me that I had an obligation.

"How's about we start a fire and eat some of this food here and then burn up the stuff you don't really need?" I paused, for effect. "Just kidding."

We transferred some of the weight from Tom's pack over to mine which, before this transfer, hadn't weighed more than twenty pounds. "Got to travel light, Tom," I said, "or else you'll be all stooped over for the next couple of weeks."

The rest of the trip went fine, except the part about the bear, which we'll save for later.

Did you ever notice there are lots of middle-aged people who seem to be all stooped over, carrying some sort of invisible load, the weight of which even shows on their faces? They're unhappy, conflicted, angry, and just "weighed down" by life. I would suspect these people haven't always been this way. They were young and happy-go-lucky at one time just like you and me.

So here's my bottom line: "Life is about Backpacks." The enjoyment of your life may depend on whether or not you are able to travel light. [Pick up last backpack.] You can travel light, but there are some things that can get into your backpack that can weigh you down and prevent you from being all you can be.

[Take out the first brick.] This brick is inscribed with the word "addictions," and refers to things that control you, steal everything about you, and slowly sap everything that is good about you until you recognize nothing good. Addictions to drugs, alcohol, pornography, and other things will destroy your best relationships and your dreams. When you are tempted to do these things, realize that no one who ever did them intended to become addicted. Don't start. Please don't put this brick in your backpack.

[Take out a second brick.] Let's call this brick "anger/conflict." These feelings may not be the individual's fault, but they are real, and people who suffer with them are under a great weight. This weight can cause them to think irrationally, to avoid doing things that they should be doing, and to settle for much less than they should settle for. This brick can cause physical and emotional illness, and insecurity that affects all personal relationships. Please don't put this brick in your backpack.

[Take out the final brick.] This final brick is inscribed with "self-absorption." It's a very heavy brick. There was a rock singer "back in our day" named Ricky Nelson, a heartthrob of teenage girls everywhere. He sang a song called "Garden Party," the main lyric of which was, "You can't please everyone, so you got to please yourself."

It began in that generation, the idea that "self" was the highest priority to be considered when evaluating pretty much everything. Is it no wonder that we have trouble finding people who can work together as a team on anything anymore, or that we refuse to participate in something if we don't get our own way? Self-absorption, and doing the best for myself, seems innocent enough, but it's an addiction all of its own. The idea that life is all about me is a happiness killer, a real back-breaker. It is the antithesis of love, which is the ultimate "brick-breaker." Love is not a feeling; it is a commitment to someone else's best interests above your own. People who are able to love travel lighter.

If you have any of these bricks in your backpack already and are feeling a little weighed down, there is hope. Just as I helped Tom carry the weight of his backpack, there are people out there who want to do the same for you. Your teachers, parents, girlfriends, boyfriends, coaches, church friends, and others want to be there for you, even though they might have some weight in their own packs as well. It is good to use our collective strength to carry each others' burdens.

My friends, thank you for not asking me to do the commencement address this year. But if I had been asked, I would have said, "Travel light; keep it simple."

God bless you, and by the way, don't forget that He is willing to carry your pack for you if you just ask.

NOTES

NOTES

NOTES

NOTES

Resources from Healthy Life Press

Unless otherwise noted on the site itself, shipping is free for all products purchased through www.healthylifepress.com.

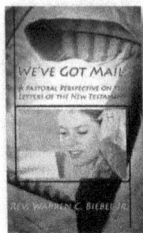

We've Got Mail: The New Testament Letters in Modern English – As Relevant Today as Ever! by Rev. Warren C. Biebel, Jr. – A modern English paraphrase of the New Testament Letters, sure to inspire in readers a loving appreciation for God's Word. (Printed book: $9.95; PDF eBook: $6.95; both together: $15.00, direct from publisher; eBook reader versions available at www.Amazon.com; www.BN.com; www.eChristian.com.)

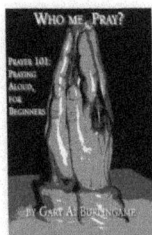

Hearth & Home – Recipes for Life, by Karey Swan (7th Edition) – Far more than a cookbook, this classic is a life book, with recipes for life as well as for great food. Karey describes how to buy and prepare from scratch a wide variety of tantalizing dishes, while weaving into the book's fabric the wisdom of the ages plus the recipe that she and her husband used to raise their kids. A great gift for Christmas or for a new bride. (Perfect Bound book [8 x 10, glossy cover]: $17.95; PDF eBook: $12.95; both together: $24.95, direct from publisher; eBook reader versions available at www.Amazon.com; www.BN.com; www.eChristian.com.)

Who Me, Pray? Prayer 101: Praying Aloud, for Beginners, by Gary A. Burlingame – *Who Me, Pray?* is a practical guide for prayer, based on Jesus' direction in "The Lord's Prayer," with examples provided for use in typical situations where you might be asked or expected to pray in public. (Printed book: $6.95; PDF eBook: $2.99; both together: $7.95, direct from publisher; eBook reader versions available at www.Amazon.com; www.BN.com; www.eChristian.com.)

The Big Black Book – What the Christmas Tree Saw, by Rev. Warren C. Biebel, Jr. – An original Christmas story, from the perspective of the Christmas tree. This little book is especially suitable for parents to read to their children at Christmas time or all year-round. (Full-color printed book: $9.95; PDF eBook: $4.95; both together: $10.95, direct from publisher; eBook reader versions available at www.Amazon.com; www.BN.com; www.eChristian.com.)

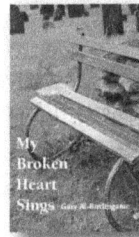

My Broken Heart Sings, the poetry of Gary Burlingame – In 1987, Gary and his wife Debbie lost their son Christopher John, at only six months of age, to a chronic lung disease. This life-changing experience gave them a special heart for helping others through similar loss and pain. (Printed book: $10.95; PDF eBook: $6.95; both together: $13.95; eBook reader versions available at www.Amazon.com; www.BN.com; www.eChristian.com.)

After Normal: One Teen's Journey Following Her Brother's Death, by Diane Aggen – Based on a journal the author kept following her younger brother's death. It offers helpful insights and understanding for teens facing a similar loss or for those who might wish to understand and help teens facing a similar loss. (Printed book: $11.95; PDF eBook: $6.95; both together: $15.00; eBook reader versions available at www.Amazon.com; www.BN.com; www.eChristian.com.)

In the Unlikely Event of a Water Landing – Lessons Learned from Landing in the Hudson River, by Andrew Jamison, MD – The author was flying standby on US Airways Flight 1549 toward Charlotte on January 15, 2009, from New York City, where he had been interviewing for a residency position. Little did he know that the next stop would be the Hudson River. Riveting and inspirational, this

book would be especially helpful for people in need of hope and encouragement. (Printed book: $8.95; PDF eBook: $6.95; both together: $12.95, direct from publisher; eBook reader versions available at www.Amazon.com; www.BN.com; www.eChristian.com.)

Finding Martians in the Dark – Everything I Needed to Know About Teaching Took Me Only 30 Years to Learn, by Dan M. Biebel – Packed with wise advice based on hard experience, and laced with humor, this book is a perfect teacher's gift year-round. Susan J. Wegmann, PhD, says, "Biebel's sardonic wit is mellowed by a genuine love for kids and teaching. . . . A Whitman-like sensibility flows through his stories of teaching, learning, and life." (Printed book: $10.95; PDF eBook: $6.95; Together: $15.00; eBook reader versions available at www.Amazon.com; www.BN.com; www.eChristian.com.)

Because We're Family and **Because We're Friends,** by Gary A. Burlingame – Sometimes things related to faith can be hard to discuss with your family and friends. These booklets are designed to be given as gifts, to help you open the door to discussing spiritual matters with family members and friends who are open to such a conversation. (Printed book: $5.95 each; PDF eBook: $4.95 each; both together: $9.95 [printed & eBook of the same title], direct from publisher; eBook reader versions available at www.Amazon.com; www.BN.com; www.eChristian.com.)

The Transforming Power of Story: How Telling Your Story Brings Hope to Others and Healing to Yourself, by Elaine Leong Eng, MD, and David B. Biebel, DMin – This book demonstrates, through multiple true life stories, how sharing one's story, especially in a group setting, can bring hope to listeners and healing to the one who shares. Individuals facing difficulties will find this book greatly encouraging. (Printed book: $14.99; PDF eBook: $9.99; both together: $19.99, direct from publisher; eBook reader versions available at www.Amazon.com; www.BN.com; www.eChristian.com.)

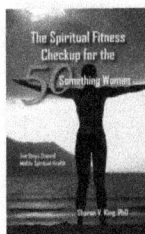

You Deserved a Better Father: Good Parenting Takes a Plan, by Robb Brandt, MD – About parenting by intention, and other lessons the author learned through the loss of his firstborn son. It is especially for parents who believe that bits and pieces of leftover time will be enough for their own children. (Printed book: $12.95 each; PDF eBook: $6.95; both together: $17.95, direct from the publisher; eBook reader versions available at www.Amazon.com; www.BN.com; www.eChristian.com.)

Jonathan, You Left Too Soon, by David B. Biebel, DMin – One pastor's journey through the loss of his son, into the darkness of depression, and back into the light of joy again, emerging with a renewed sense of mission. (Printed book: $12.95; PDF eBook: $5.99; both together: $15.00, direct from publisher; eBook reader versions available at www.Amazon.com; www.BN. com; www.eChristian.com.)

The Spiritual Fitness Checkup for the 50-Something Woman, by Sharon V. King, PhD – Following the stages of a routine medical exam, the author describes ten spiritual fitness "checkups" midlife women can conduct to assess their spiritual health and tone up their relationship with God. Each checkup consists of the author's personal reflections, a Scripture reference for meditation, and a "Spiritual Pulse Check," with exercises readers can use for personal application. (Printed book: $8.95; PDF eBook: $6.95; both together: $12.95, direct from publisher; eBook reader versions available at www.Amazon.com; www.BN.com; www.eChristian.com.)

The Other Side of Life – Over 60? God Still Has a Plan for You, by Rev. Warren C. Biebel, Jr. – Drawing on biblical examples and his 60-plus years of pastoral experience, Rev. Biebel helps older (and younger) adults understand God's view of aging and the rich life available to everyone who seeks a deeper relationship with God as they age. Rev. Biebel explains how to: Identify God's ongoing plan for your life; Rely on faith to manage the anxieties of aging; Form positive, supportive relationships; Cultivate patience; Cope with new technologies; Develop spiritual integrity; Understand the effects of dementia; Develop a Christ-centered perspective of aging. (Printed book: $10.95; PDF eBook: $6.95; both together: $15.00, direct from publisher; eBook reader versions available at www.Amazon.com; www.BN.com; www.eChristian.com.)

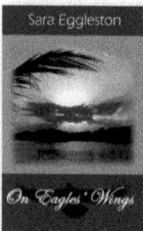

My Faith, My Poetry, by Gary A. Burlingame – This unique book of Christian poetry is actually two in one. The first collection of poems, *A Day in the Life*, explores a working parent's daily journey of faith. The reader is carried from morning to bedtime, from "In the Details," to "I Forgot to Pray," back to "Home Base," and finally to "Eternal Love Divine." The second collection of poems, *Come Running*, is wonder, joy, and faith wrapped up in words that encourage and inspire the mind and the heart. (Printed book: $10.95; PDF eBook: $6.95; both together: $13.95, direct from publisher; eBook reader versions available at www.Amazon.com; www.BN.com; www.eChristian.com.)

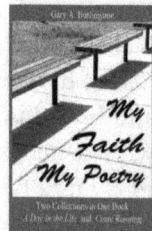

On Eagles' Wings, by Sara Eggleston – One woman's life journey from idyllic through chaotic to joy, carried all the way by the One who has promised to never leave us nor forsake us. Remarkable, poignant, moving, and inspiring, this autobiographical account will help many who are facing difficulties that seem too great to overcome or even bear at all. It is proof that Isaiah 40:31 is as true today as when it was penned, "But they that wait upon the

LORD shall renew their strength; they shall mount up with wings as eagles; they shall run, and not be weary; and they shall walk, and not faint." (Printed book: $14.95; PDF eBook: $8.95; both together: $22.95, direct from publisher; eBook reader versions available at www.Amazon.com; www.BN.com; www.eChristian.com.)

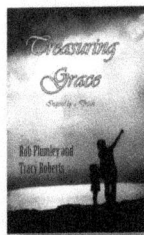

Richer Descriptions, by Gary A. Burlingame – A unique and handy manual, covering all <u>nine</u> human senses in seven chapters, for Christian speakers and writers. Exercises and a speaker's checklist equip speakers to engage their audiences in a richer experience. Writing examples and a writer's guide help writers bring more life to the characters and scenes of their stories. Bible references encourage a deeper appreciation of being created by God for a sensory existence. (Printed book: $15.95; PDF eBook: $8.95; both together: $22.95, direct from publisher; eBook reader versions available at www.Amazon.com; www.BN.com; www.eChristian.com.)

Treasuring Grace, by Rob Plumley and Tracy Roberts – This novel was inspired by a dream. Liz Swanson's life isn't quite what she'd imagined, but she considers herself lucky. She has a good husband, beautiful children, and fulfillment outside of her home through volunteer work. On some days she doesn't even notice the dull ache in her heart. While she's preparing for their summer kickoff at Lake George, the ache disappears and her sudden happiness is mistaken for anticipation of their weekend. However, as the family heads north, there are clouds on the horizon that have nothing to do with the weather. Only Liz's daughter, who's found some of her mother's hidden journals, has any idea what's wrong. But by the end of the weekend, there will be no escaping the truth or its painful buried secrets. (Printed: $12.95; PDF eBook: $7.95; both together: $19.95, direct from publisher; eBook reader versions available at www.Amazon.com; www.BN.com; www.eChristian.com.)

Life's A Symphony, by Mary Z. Smith – When Kate Spence Cooper receives the news that her husband, Jack, has been killed in the war, she and her young son Jeremy move back to Crawford Wood, Tennessee to be closer to family. Since Jack's death Kate feels that she's lost trust in everyone, including God. Will she ever find her way back to the only One whom she can always depend upon? And what about Kate's match making brother, Chance? The cheeky man has other ideas on how to bring happiness into his sister's life once more. (Printed book: $12.95; PDF eBook: $7.95; both together: $19.95, direct from publisher; eBook reader versions available at www.Amazon.com; www.BN.com; www.eChristian.com.)

Your Mind at Its Best – 40 Ways To Keep Your Brain Sharp, by David B. Biebel, DMin; James E. Dill, MD; and, Bobbie Dill, RN – Everyone wants their mind to function at high levels throughout life. In 40 easy-to-understand chapters, readers will discover a wide variety of tips and tricks to keep their minds sharp. Synthesizing science and self-help, *Your Mind at Its Best* makes fascinating neurological discoveries understandable and immediately applicable to readers of any age. (Printed book: $13.99.)

From Orphan to Physician – The Winding Path, by Chun-Wai Chan, MD – From the foreword: "In this book, Dr. Chan describes how his family escaped to Hong Kong, how they survived in utter poverty, and how he went from being an orphan to graduating from Harvard Medical School and becoming a cardiologist. The writing is fluent, easy to read and understand. The sequence of events is realistic, emotionally moving, spiritually touching, heartwarming, and thought provoking. The book illustrates . . . how one must have faith in order to walk through life's winding path." (Printed book: $14.95; PDF eBook: $8.95; both together: $22.95, direct from publisher; eBook reader versions available at www.Amazon.com; www.BN.com; www.eChristian.com.)

12 Parables, by Wayne Faust – Timeless Christian stories about doubt, fear, change, grief, and more. Using tight, entertaining prose, professional musician and comedy performer Wayne Faust manages to deal with difficult concepts in a simple, straightforward way. These are stories you can read aloud over and over—to your spouse, your family, or in a group setting. Packed with emotion and just enough mystery to keep you wondering, while providing lots of points to ponder and discuss when you're through, these stories relate the gospel in the tradition of the greatest speaker of parables the world has ever known, who appears in them often. (Printed book: $14.95; PDF eBook: $8.95; both together: $22.95, direct from publisher; eBook reader versions available at www. Amazon.com; www.BN.com; www.eChristian.com.)

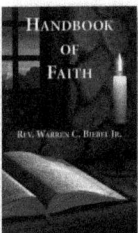

The Answer is Always "Jesus," by Aram Haroutunian, who gave children's sermons for 15 years at a large church in Golden, Colorado—well over 500 in all. This book contains 74 of his most unforgettable presentations—due to the children's responses. Pastors, homeschoolers, parents who often lead family devotions, or other storytellers will find these stories, along with comments about props and how to prepare and present them, an invaluable asset in reconnecting with the simplest, most profound truths of Scripture, and then to envision how best to communicate these so even a child can understand them. (Printed book: $12.95; PDF eBook: $8.95; both together: $19.95, direct from publisher; eBook reader versions available at www.Amazon.com; www.BN.com; www.eChristian.com.)

Handbook of Faith, by Rev. Warren C. Biebel, Jr. – The *New York Times World 2011 Almanac* claimed that there are 2 billion, 200 thousand Christians in the world, with "Christians" being defined as "followers of Christ." The original 12 followers of Christ changed the world; indeed, they changed the history of the world. So this author, a pastor with over 60 years' experience, poses and answers this logical question: "If there are so many 'Christians' on this planet, why are they so relatively ineffective in serving the One they claim to follow?" Answer: Because, unlike Him, they do not know and trust the Scriptures, implicitly. This little volume will help you do that. (Printed book: $8.95; PDF eBook: $6.95; both together: $13.95, direct from publisher; eBook reader versions available at www.Amazon.com; www.BN.com; www.eChristian.com.)

Pieces of My Heart, by David L. Wood – Eighty-two lessons from normal everyday life. David's hope is that these stories will spark thoughts about God's constant involvement and intervention in our lives and stir a sense of how much He cares about every detail that is important to us. The piece missing represents his son, Daniel, who died in a fire shortly before his first birthday. (Printed book: $16.95; PDF eBook: $8.95; both together: $24.95, direct from publisher; eBook reader versions available at www.Amazon.com; www.BN.com; www.eChristian.com.)

☞ PLEASE NOTE:

Prices listed in this catalog may have been updated since these pages were printed. Current prices are indicated on our website: *www.healthylifepress.com*. Individuals or retail outlets that wish more information may contact us at: *info@healthylifepress.com.*

Dream House, by Justa Carpenter – Written by a New England builder of several hundred homes, the idea for this book came to him one day as he was driving that came to him one day as was driving from one job site to another. He pulled over and recorded it so he would remember it, and now you will remember it, too, if you believe, as he

does, that ". . . He who has begun a good work in you will complete it until the day of Jesus Christ." (Printed book: $8.95; PDF eBook: $6.95; both together: $13.95, direct from publisher; eBook reader versions available at www.Amazon.com; www.BN.com; www.eChristian.com.)

A Simply Homemade Clean, by homesteader Lisa Barthuly – "Somewhere along the path, it seems we've lost our gumption, the desire to make things ourselves," says the author. "Gone are the days of 'do it yourself.' Really . . . why bother? There are a slew of retailers just waiting for us with anything and everything we could need; packaged up all pretty, with no thought or effort required. It is the manifestation of 'progress' . . . right?" I don't buy that!" Instead, Lisa describes how to make safe and effective cleansers for home, laundry, and body right in your own home. This saves money and avoids exposure to harmful chemicals often found in commercially produced cleansers. (Printed book: $12.99; PDF eBook: $6.95; both together: $17.95, direct from publisher; **full-color printed book: $16.99**, only at www.healthylifepress.com; eBook reader versions available at www.Amazon.com; www.BN.com; www.eChristian.com.)

HEALTHY LIFE PRESS DISTRIBUTION

Most Healthy Life Press books are available worldwide online and through bookstores. Distribution is primarily through CreateSpace.com. Bookstores may order at a discount directly from the publisher. For details, e-mail us at: info@healthylifepress.com. Our ePublications are available through *Amazon.com* (Kindle), *BN.com* (Nook), and for all commercial readers through *eChristian.com*. All resources are available via *www.healthylifepress.com*.

RECOMMENDED RESOURCES –
PRO-LIFE DVD SERIES

SEE WWW.HEALTHYLIFEPRESS.COM (SELECT "DVD")
FOR TRAILERS AND SPECIAL COMBINATION PRICING

Eyewitness 2 (Public School Version) – This DVD has been used in many public schools. It is a fascinating journey through 38 weeks of pregnancy, showing developing babies via cutting edge digital ultrasound technology. Separate chapters allow viewing distinct segments individually. (List Price: $34.95; Sale Price: $24.95.)

Window To The Womb (2 DVD Disc Set) Disc 1: Ian Donald (1910-1987) "A Prophetic Legacy;" Disc 2: "A Journey from Death To Life" (50 min) – Includes history of sonography and its increasing impact against abortion—more than 80% of expectant parents who "see" their developing baby choose for life. Perfect for counseling and education in Pregnancy Centers, Christian schools, homeschools, and churches. (List: $49.95; Sale: $34.95.)

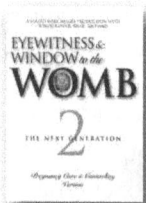

Window To the Womb (Pregnancy Care & Counseling Version) – Facts about fetal development, abortion complications, post-abortion syndrome, and healing. Separate chapters allow selection of specialized presentations to accommodate the needs and time constraints of their situations. (List: $34.95; Sale: $24.95.)

Unless otherwise noted on the site itself, shipping is free for all products purchased through www.healthylifepress.com.

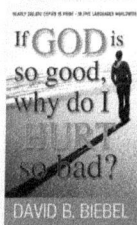

If God Is So Good, Why Do I Hurt So Bad?, by David B. Biebel, DMin – In this best-selling classic (over 200,000 copies in print worldwide, in five languages) on the subject of loss and renewal, first published in 1989, the author comes alongside people in pain, and shows the way through and beyond it, to joy again. This book has proven helpful to those who are struggling and to those who wish to understand and help. (Printed book: $12.95; PDF eBook: $8.95; both together: $19.95, direct from publisher; eBook reader versions available at www.Amazon.com; www.BN.com; www.eChristian.com.)

52 Ways to Feel Great Today, by David B. Biebel, DMin, James E. Dill, MD, and Bobbie Dill, RN – **Increase Your Vitality, Improve your Outlook.** Simple, fun, inexpensive things you can do to increase your vitality and improve your outlook. Why live an "ordinary" life when you could be experiencing the extraordinary? Don't settle for good enough when "great" is such a short stretch away. Make today great! (Printed book: $14.99.)

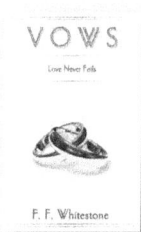

VOWS, a Romantic novel by F. F. Whitestone – When the police cruiser pulled up to the curb outside, Faith Framingham's heart skipped a beat, for she could see that Chuck, who should have been driving, was not in the vehicle. Chuck's partner, Sandy, stepped out slowly. Sandy's pursed lips and ashen face spoke volumes. Faith waited by the front door, her hands clasped tightly, to counter the fact that her mind was already reeling. "Love never fails." A compelling story. (Printed book: $12.99; PDF eBook: $9.99; both together, $19.99, direct from publisher; eBook reader versions available at www.Amazon.com; www.BN.com; www.eChristian.com.)

New Light on Depression, a CBA Gold Medallion winner, by David B. Biebel, DMin, and Harold Koenig, MD – The most exhaustive Christian resource on a subject that is more common than we might wish. Hope for those with depression and help for those who love them. (Printed book: $15.00.)

The A to Z Guide To Healthier Living, by David B. Biebel, DMin, James E. Dill, MD, and Bobbie Dill, RN – You'll find great info on: avoiding fad diets, being kind to your GI tract, building healthy bones, finding contentment, getting a good night's sleep, keeping your relationships strong, simplifying your life, staying creative, and much more. (Printed book: 12.99.)

The Secret of Singing Springs, by Monte Swan – One Colorado family's treasure-hunting adventure along the trail of Jesse James. *The Secret of Singing Springs* is written to capture for children and their parents the spirit of the hunt—the hunt for treasure as in God's Truth, which is the objective of walking the Way of Wisdom that is described in the book of Proverbs. (Printed book: $12.99; PDF eBook: $9.99; both together: $19.99, direct from publisher; eBook reader versions at www.Amazon.com; www.BN.com; www.eChristian.com.) **NEWLY RELEASED IN 2013.**

God Loves You Circle, by Michelle Johnson – Daily inspiration for your deeper walk with Christ. This collection of short stories of Christian living will make you laugh, make you cry, but most of all make you contemplate—the meaning and value of walking with the Master moment-by-moment, day-by-day. (**Full-color book: $17.95**; full-color PDF eBook: $9.99; both together: $23.99, direct from the publisher; eBook reader versions available at www.Amazon.com; www.BN.com; www.eChristian.com. **NEWLY RELEASED IN 2013.**

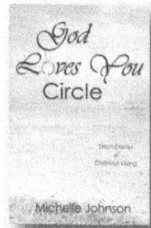

MORE NEW BOOKS FROM HEALTHY LIFE PRESS - 2013

Our God-Given Senses, by Gary A. Burlingame – Did you know humans have NINE senses? The Bible draws on these senses to reveal spiritual truth. We are to taste and see that the Lord is a good. We are to carry the fragrance of Christ. Our faith is produced upon hearing. Jesus asked Thomas to touch him. God created us for a sensory experience and that is what you will find in this book. (Printed book: $12.99; PDF eBook: $9.99; both together: $19.99, direct from publisher; eBook reader versions available at www.Amazon. com; www.BN.com; www.eChristian.com. Available Spring 2013.)

I AM – Transformed in Him – by Diana Burg and Kim Tapfer, a meditative women's Bible study of the I AM statements of Christ in two 6-week volumes or one 12-week volume. Throughout this six week study you will begin to unearth the treasure trove of riches that are found within God's name, I AM WHO I AM. (Printed book: $12.99; PDF eBook: $9.99; both together: $19.99, direct from publisher; eBook reader versions available at www. Amazon.com; www.BN.com; www.eChristian.com.)

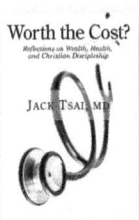

Worth the Cost?, by Jack Tsai, MD – The author was happily on his way to obtaining the American Dream until he decided to take seriously Jesus' command to "Come, follow me." Join him as he explores the cost of medical education and Christian discipleship. Planning to serve God in your future vocation? Take care that your desires do not get side-tracked by the false promises of this world. What you should be doing now so when you are done with your training you will still want to serve God. (Printed book: $12.99, PDF eBook: $9.99; both together: $19.99, direct from publisher; eBook reader versions available: www.Amazon.com; www.BN.com; www.eChristian.com.)

Nature: God's Second Book – An Essential Link to Restoring Your Personal Health and Wellness: Body, Mind, and Spirit, by Elvy P. Rolle – An inspirational book that looks at nature across the chronological and life seasons. It uses the biblical Emmaus Journey as an analogy for life's journey, and offers ideas for using nature appreciation and exploration to reduce life's stresses. The author shares her personal story of how she came to grips with this concept after three trips to the emergency room. (Full-color printed book: $12.99, direct from publisher only; PDF eBook $8.99; both together: $16.99, direct from publisher only; eBook reader versions available at www.Amazon.com; www. BN.com; www.eChristian.com.)

ABOUT HEALTHY LIFE PRESS

Healthy Life Press was founded with a primary goal of helping previously unpublished authors to get their works to market, and to reissue worthy, previously published works that were no longer available. Our mission is to help people toward optimal vitality by providing resources promoting physical, emotional, spiritual, and relational health as viewed from a Christian perspective. We see health as a verb, and achieving optimal health as a process—a crucial process for followers of Christ if we are to love the Lord with all our heart, soul, mind, AND strength, and our neighbors as ourselves—for as long as He leaves us here. We are a collaborative and cooperative small Christian publisher. We share costs/we share proceeds.

For information about publishing with us, e-mail: healthylifepress@aol.com.